MYLES AWAY FROM DUBLIN

By the Same Author

—

THE BEST OF MYLES
AT SWIM-TWO-BIRDS
THE HARD LIFE
THE DALKEY ARCHIVE
THE THIRD POLICEMAN
THE POOR MOUTH
STORIES AND PLAYS
KEATS AND CHAPMAN and THE BROTHER
THE HAIR OF THE DOGMA
FURTHER CUTTINGS FROM CRUISKEEN LAWN

Myles na Gopaleen
(Flann O'Brien)

MYLES AWAY FROM DUBLIN

being a selection from the
column written for
The Nationalist and Leinster Times,
Carlow,
under the name of
George Knowall

Selected and introduced by
Martin Green

The Lilliput Press
Dublin

First published by Granada Publishing 1985
This edition published in 2012 by
THE LILLIPUT PRESS
62–63 Sitric Road, Arbour Hill, Dublin 7, Ireland
www.lilliputpress.ie

ISBN 978 1 84351 265 3

A CIP record for this is available from The British Library

The Lilliput Press receives financial assistance from
An Chomhairle Ealaion / The Arts Council of Ireland

Printed and bound in Sweden by ScandBook AB

Introduction

Nothing is easy to pin down about the author of this book, particularly his various *personae*, or the names he adopted for them when appearing in print. For my purpose it is simplest to call him Myles, as Myles na Gopaleen was the name he is best remembered by for his excursions into the columns of newspapers. However, this is not simply a supplementary volume to *The Best of Myles*, which was a selection from 'Cruiskeen Lawn', the column he wrote for the *Irish Times* over a period of twenty-five years, because in writing an entirely new column, 'Bones of Contention', for the *Nationalist and Leinster Times* he adopted not only a new name, that of George Knowall, he also took on a new *persona*, that of a quizzical and enquiring humorist who might be found in a respectable public house in Carlow. It had been my intention originally to make a selection from both the *Nationalist* and the *Southern Star*, Skibbereen, but the John James Doe of 'A Weekly Look Around' never managed to become a person in his own right, and the column was patchy and tailed off after the first year and barely saw out a second, albeit there were one or two typical Mylesian pieces. To have included them here would have been a disservice to the man who addressed himself faithfully to his Carlovian readers.

One of Myles's remarkable achievements as a columnist was that of consistency supported by a spring of imaginative energy; for whatsoever the vicissitudes of life generally, and those attaching to people in and around newspapers in particular, he maintained an extraordinary output right up to and including the year of his death in 1966. Another remarkable strength was the quality of his writing. Homer nods, but Myles's delight in language never leaves him and whether he is writing on the seasonal and annual events, the weather or the Dublin Horse Show, he is always able to make something fresh. To write well is not easy, nor is it a gift like perfect pitch; it is difficult and demanding. No one could pick his way round the hazards of journalistic clichés with such deftness as Myles, nor turn them to such good use when it suited his need, as in the 'Myles na Gopaleen Catechism of Cliché', with which he rewarded the devoted followers of 'Cruiskeen Lawn'.

The *persona* he presented to the people of Carlow, under the name of George Knowall, was different from the one who addressed the plain people of Ireland in the *Irish Times*, yet his felicitous use of language, his delight in words, and his uncanny ability to see through humbug and cant were employed to the same end.

To those admirers of Myles who know a little about his life, he drops various autobiographical hints that can be picked up and enjoyed. Since what happens to him is as much grist to his mill as are the absurdities recorded in the daily papers, we nearly always get a bulletin about his health when upset, and a gentle swipe at the medical profession and the undignified absurdity of being in hospital when the misfortune arises, as it does periodically in the following pages. We are treated variously to a broken leg, influenza (with a note about a lady who survived an operation when young and spent the rest of her life talking about and embellishing the event), vaccination, a phantom heart-attack wrongly diagnosed, convalescence, hospital treatment, and the operation that probably concerned his last illness. Doubtless he would have agreed that there is only one fatal illness, the one that kills you, and would have used this unfashionable medical apophthegm as a text. Certainly his absence from the pages of the *Nationalist* was of long duration preceding the appearance of the operation piece, but nowhere is the sharpness blunted or his verbal enthusiasm dampened in any of the pieces he wrote after his return.

The Myles of the *Nationalist* is eminently sensible and

proclaims himself born into a lower middle class family, something that 'connotes, of course, ultra respectability, carefulness amounting to perhaps contempt of the real poor . . .'. And it is from this position that he writes in these pages, though he personally was never victim to the hypocrisies inherent in that position. He delights in curious and arcane knowledge, though he has no time for 'facts' as purveyed say in radio quiz programmes or in the *Guinness Book of Records*, a 'book full of extraordinary allegations, for the veracity of which no source or proof is given.' When he himself takes an interest in something, such as the word 'dowse', and follows it through all its meanings and implications, we get a truly adventurous and delightful journey with a courteous and attentive guide.

The Myles of the *Nationalist* is erudite, urbane and informative and on the whole a country cousin to his metropolitan self. I have seen no reason to arrange the material here under subject headings, since he treated his readers with such attentiveness that the pieces are better read chronologically, as they were published, one subject written about once being taken up again at a later date. The provincial Myles was always mindful that his readership was a loyal and local one and he goes out of his way to address Carlovians as such, taking the trouble as often as not to allude to recently published matter in a previous edition, whether an article or an editorial comment. One such, a feature on agriculture, encourages – and this against the tide that took Ireland into the Common Market – a gentle attack on agriculture as being 'alien and un-Irish', claiming that in a study of Irish poetry from 1500 to 1750 there is no mention of the subject, save allusions to pasturage, hunting and the keeping of domestic livestock, including deer. Normally, the supplementary matter in a newspaper which devotes a special feature to a subject supports the burden, its central aim being to attract advertising, and it would appear that Myles was as much a licensed jester in the *Nationalist* as he was in the

Irish Times. Indeed, the delight we take in a humorous columnist, from Beachcomber to Peter Simple, is that he can take the mind away from the ponderous absurdities of the editorial and the obsessional attention to the topicalities of the day, and enable us to see things in a truer perspective, for comedy is as much at the heart of the matter as is tragedy, and likewise as durable. Not many columnists can justify publication in book form.

As the George Knowall of the *Nationalist* is a country relation of the Myles of Dublin, so they are both part of a composite human being who wrote those extraordinary works *The Third Policeman*, *At Swim-Two-Birds* and the play *Faustus Kelly*. For the two former he chose the name of Flann O'Brien and it is difficult sometimes to reconcile even two different Flann O'Briens as one and the same author. There *are* tides in the affairs of men, surmount them as we may, that do have a profound influence on the direction a man's life takes.

James Joyce didn't let World War I interfere with his single-minded literary endeavour, while it involved the whole of Europe in carnage and massacre and dominated the lives or fortunes of many other writers, both Irish and English; but World War II forestalled the appearance of *The Third Policeman* by over twenty-five years and made it a posthumous publication. There are various ironies in the life of the author that are almost as mysterious and other-worldly as the events in *At Swim-Two-Birds* and *The Third Policeman* and who knows what might have happened had the latter book been published rightfully as it was written, immediately after *At Swim-Two-Birds*. I myself have unearthed two characters in *At Swim* who originally appeared in the pages of a French writer, Alphonse Allais, whose work was only translated into English and published here a couple of years ago.

In bringing this selection together from the columns of the *Nationalist* the intention has not been to search out and garner more of Myles for the sake of it, but to show again that as one more facet of this many-sided writer appears, there is the certain knowledge that no one will ever be able to see the whole at any one given moment. He was a man who disappeared from his own photographs, knowing that a photograph is not a prophecy, but a moment, an expression frozen in time. His future is in his writing, and this volume is part of that future.

Martin Green
Newlyn, March 1984

Note

The pieces collected here were first published in the *Nationalist and Leinster Times*, Carlow, between 1960 and 1966, under the heading of 'Bones of Contention'.

The fiercest of them all

For a reason not clear at all, humans impute to animals motives and behaviours quite alien to them; it is not easy to work out the inter-relation of the man-animal kingdom. Notionally, man is the ascendant and dominant class. Is he in fact, though?

The red setter lying at the fire knows every word I say. And if you were to lay a finger on me, without even going to the trouble of pretending you are going to hit me, he would spring up and tear you asunder.

Although cats are not strictly speaking domesticated at all, preserving a private life of their own (particularly its nocturnal side) they are faultless time-keepers inasmuch as they show up on the dot at meal times and in cold weather they take the fullest advantage of fires. In matters of cleanliness indoors they are most fastidious *and* it is fallacy that they are afraid of dogs. A cat on the war-path will terrify any dog, though a chase is often conceded as a matter of exercise and fresh air.

We attribute almost limitless intelligence to monkeys, no doubt because of their anthropoid appearance and the human skill with which they drink tea and smoke cigarettes. Elephants we consider very wise and admire the gentleness with which they behave, notwithstanding that they weigh several tons.

What of the rat? He is not a very personable fellow and often carries a selection of typhus and bubonic germs in his fur coat. All the same, I confess I cannot withhold from him a certain measure of approval. His cunning is proverbial and must be highly commended, if only expressed in his feat of remaining alive at all. Probably no creature in this part of the world has so many mortal enemies. Not only are dogs, cats and humans after him but he has special enemies such as the hedgehog. I have read that it is estimated that there are

8,000,000 rats in Ireland alone, a great number of them natives of Dublin.

The Major Fauna

Few of us have soldiered in the Far East and for that reason have only the most perfunctory acquaintance with the great beasts such as the lion, tiger and leopard. The snake family we hardly know at all, thanks no doubt to St Patrick. Our nearest bears are probably in Siberia, crocodiles infest the foetid swamps of India and the Abominable Snowman is still tramping around the slopes of the Himalayas. Apart from indigenous minor fauna – the rabbit, the hare, the goat and the deer – that seems to be about the limit of our knowledge of the Wild, a compound of snooping, hearsay and Walt Disney. I keep away deliberately from the subject of salmon for therein we have a mishmash of poaching, gunplay and perjury. In a way, we can claim to be innocent enough.

We live with Nature, hoping that modest benefit may accrue to us without undue exertion; we give thanks when a fat grouse dies from heart failure at our feet, and with resignation we accept the fact that pheasants cannot expect to live forever.

But these notes of mine today are directed to asking the reader to name the most ferocious animal in this part of the world. The badger or the bull? Neither. The dog whose fangs drip with hydrophobia? No. Man himself? Hardly. Quoting from two books I have read, let me name the brute.

It is the shrew. The shrew is a little thing weighing about half an ounce, in appearance very like a small mouse except that he has a long pointed snout and a shorter tail.

Mind This Fellow

Naturalists are agreed that, considering his size and needs, nothing in the whole animal kingdom can compare with the common shrew in savagery and voracity. Tigers are clumsy messers in comparison and they always pick a smaller animal when in search of prey.

The shrew is permanently in a towering rage and, notwithstanding the fact that in his last meal of a few hours ago he ate three times his own weight, he is perpetually a martyr to hunger. If nothing better can be found, he will kill and eat another shrew – murder and repast taking merely a matter of seconds. But he has no hesitation in attacking, killing and trying to eat the whole of a rat, who must look mammoth in proportion to himself. Part of his armoury is that, apart from the ability to unleash a filthy smell, his tiny biting apparatus contains a glandular poison which can paralyse victims almost no matter what their size. His appetite is quite insatiable, his unending rage is quite startling and by the time he is 15 months old he has eaten himself to death. He is afraid of absolutely nothing except the possibility of doing without his dinner.

Should the Irish farmer beware of the shrew and even set shrew-traps? He should not be, for the shrew eats snails, slugs and every manner of insect while awaiting some larger and more succulent dish. But the question does not arise, for there are no shrews at all in Ireland. St Patrick again!

Some notes on playing the game

I was startled to read recently in the giant Sunday issue of a San Francisco paper the casual statement that handball is the national game of Ireland. It made me think generally about games. What is a national game or, for that matter, what is a *game*?

The dictionaries are a bit vague here. A game is said to be any amusement or sport, or a contest played for recreation or as an exhibition of skill. It seems also that the word 'game' meaning creatures other than what is meat, fish or poultry and which you go after with a gun is really the same word, as also is gaming in the sense of gambling.

It is not so easy to decide within those meanings what a national game is. In western continental Europe it is probably true to say that the national game of most countries is soccer. But would it be true to say that the national game of Spain is bull-fighting, or is bull-fighting a game at all? Is boxing a game? The Swiss spend a lot of their time skiing and otherwise cavorting on snow and ice. Could that be called their national game? And if one were to get into an acrimonious argument with a member of the Japanese nation, one might suddenly find oneself in mid-air and then slammed to the floor with a shattering crash – merely as a result of participating in the national game of ju-ju. Deciding on the US national game would take some thought. Baseball comes to mind but there is also great emphasis on basket-ball, ice hockey, football and . . . handball.

With the Ancients

The founders of our civilisation took their games very seriously and left a heritage in the matter, as is evidenced by the fact that this year there is world-wide participation in the Olympic Games.

The Greeks called their games *agones*, which are mentioned in the *Iliad*. They were by no means exclusively recreational athletic exercises but were part of religious observances. Games were held as part of funeral rites or in thanks to the gods for some military triumph or a disaster averted. Olympia was a naturally enclosed place not far from Athens, lined with statues of great athletes of the past and surmounted by a chryselephantine statue of the Olympian Zeus by the famous sculptor Pheidias. The games in their ritualistic aspect were evidence of the refinement of the Greeks as they took the place of the savage custom elsewhere of slaughtering slaves and captives on the grave of any important man who died, as an offering to the gods.

What were the events of the games? The *foot race* was important, being usually decided in heats and run over about 200 yards. For a time there was also a race in heavy armour, highly recommended by Plato as great training for the army. Next came *wrestling*, not very different from the all-in stuff of today. Then came the *pentathlon*, a miscellaneous 5-game contest which included the long jump. Tall tales were in fashion even then, and the record shows a wonder-man named Phayllus credited with a jump of 35 feet. I am told this is quite impossible but there may have been something special in the Hellenic air of those days. There were boxing contests similar to those of today but subject to the condition that a boxer who killed his opponent, unless by sheer accident, not only was disqualified but was severely punished. (That is a condition we do not insist on today.) *Chariot-racing*, a very dangerous event, was also very important and as many as 40 chariots taking part in the same race. And that was about the lot.

The Decadent Romans

The Roman games, or *ludi*, veered away from the good clean fun of the Greeks. Everything was on a vaster scale and the Colosseum, which still stands substantially in Rome, was reputed to seat 350,000 people. These games also had at least a nominal religious significance. Chariot races were very popular, the war-cars being often hauled by as many as four horses. The coarseness of the people's taste was shown by their love of the aspect of the games known as *venatio* – the baiting of wild animals in the arena, setting them on one another or on criminals and slaves. Remote provinces were ransacked for rare and ferocious animals. Lions, tigers, giraffes, elephants and crocodiles were on frequent display; on one occasion Pompey provided 600 lions and on one occasion of the celebration of a victory of Trajan, 11,000 wild animals were butchered in the arena. Julius Caesar himself is credited with having invented bull-fighting. In due time Christians were thrown to the lions but the 'normal' prize attraction was the gladiators who had to fight to the death and who were chased out on to the arena with red hot irons where they showed reluctance or fear. There were even women gladiators, being matched with dwarfs.

Our Irish Game

We started, however, with handball. It seems beyond dispute that the true Irish national game is hurling, for we are told that Cuchulainn could not undertake any journey without pucking a ball ahead of him and following it. (The true roots of golf may be there.)

It seems true, however, that handball did originate in Ireland about a thousand years ago. Today it is one of the most popular games for men in the United States. The first man to work out the modern scientific system of play in the 1850s was a Tipperaryman with the engaging name of William Baggs. Another pioneer was named David Browning and in 1885 John Lawlor won the Irish championship. In 1887 Lawlor was matched with Casey of the US for a purse of $1,000 for the best out of 21 games, 10 to be played in Cork and 11 in the US. Lawlor won six games in Cork but Casey won seven straight in New York and thus won the match.

It seems a pity that handball is not encouraged more in the schools here for, the capital cost of the alley apart, it must be one of the cheapest as well as one of the most vigorous sports imaginable.

The bridge at Athlone

Up to ten or twelve years ago – how vague one can be on comparatively recent happenings! – an arriving diplomat would be greeted at airport or railway station in Ireland by a detachment of what the natives insisted on calling the Blue Hussars. These were ordinary army men but they were mounted and wore a blue dress uniform which was set off with certain gay trimmings.

Cynics murmured about comic opera police and some sourpusses asked how much this nonsense was costing the taxpayer but the people in general liked those boys in blue and admired their glistening horses; if an objector pointed out that they did not pay or were a dead loss, the answer was 'Does the army itself pay?' What army on earth does pay? If a country must have one (as apparently every country must) why not make it worth looking at on ceremonial occasions and get away from this awful monotony of nameless men in battle-dress and steel helmets marching endlessly away to God knows where?

Suddenly the Blue Hussars were abolished. No official reason was given. Possibly some civil servant, suffering from his occupational disease of indigestion, found that their extinction would save the country £20 and that maybe another five could be made by flogging their uniforms to the Queen's Theatre. That sort of reasoning is contemptible.

A Silly Remark

A few weeks ago in a restaurant I heard a member of a group which I would describe as of the student class point scornfully to a paper and say: 'They can't even write or print correctly. They call the Costume Barracks at Athlone the Custume Barracks.'

That rather shallow of military dress, between the garb of the Blue Hussars and the defenders at Athlone, is my excuse for referring here to the Custume Barracks at Athlone. When a student myself, I tried to write an extended essay on Sergeant Custume and remember being deeply shocked at the way any information about him was so diffused and scanty. I cannot reveal, even now, his Christian name. There is no consecutive account of him in existence in print and among the scattered data is the *Memoirs of King James II*, to be seen in some libraries, and *A Diary of the Siege of Athlone*, not to be seen in any library except the British Museum, where it is an unpublished manuscript, author described as 'Engineer Officer' but otherwise unidentified.

The Critical Bridge

Some people insist on identifying an important stage in Irish history with the Battle of the Boyne; decisive as that was, the Battle of the Shannon should not be ignored. It was there that Sergeant Custume and ten unnamed comrades gave their lives in a vain but very courageous gesture.

The year was 1691 and the Jacobite war here was coming to a climax. The Irish armies, under Maxwell, a Scot, had been driven across the Shannon at Athlone but were encamped in good order on the western bank of the river. The stout masonry bridge which they seemed to command consisted of nine arches plus, at the western side, a drawbridge with a tower or castle nearby, this bridge separating them from the Williamite armies under Ginkel. Clearly it was Ginkel's job to take the bridge and cross the river.

On this apparently simple situation, any records I looked up are surprisingly vague. The Irish on the Connacht side broke the bridge but it is not clear whether they demolished part of the masonry structure or simply raised the drawbridge. The two forces were roughly equal except that the Williamites had great superiority in artillery and had probably attacked the tower housing the machinery operating the drawbridge and disabled it. In any event, Ginkel's army had to cross the Shannon using a bridge, part of which was missing.

After a bombardment lasting 98 hours, his men started across the existing part of the bridge in the middle of a June night, carrying massive beams and planks to span the broken part of the bridge. So skilful and stealthy were they that they had their timbers in position before the defenders knew exactly what was happening; the confusion was probably due to the non-stop exchange of gunfire across the river.

It was here that Sergeant Custume came to notice. He went to his superior officer and volunteered, with ten men who accompanied him, to tear down the shaky structure of planks. He was given permission to attempt what seemed a quite impossible task, for the timbers were massive and gunfire at the spot was unrelenting. It may seem comic to add that Sergeant Custume and his little company wore armour but the detail is important inasmuch as the rifle, with its revolving missile of great penetration, had not yet been invented and bullets from straight-bore muskets bounced off armour. Custume and his men did the apparently impossible job, and all were eventually killed. Another company which took their place were likewise wiped out.

In a strict military sense, it was all a waste of blood and time. Yet I wish the young fellow I mentioned at the start would learn the considerable difference between the words Custume and Costume.

Uprooting, upheaval,
a coming havoc?

I suppose it is a commonplace to say that life is a series of crises, all fraught with danger. Three familiar points of crisis are birth, marriage, death. But there are many, many others, some of them quite unexpected, some very frightening. Some seem even pleasurable. But you never know what tomorrow's day will bring. Maybe it's just as well.

I came almost literally to the crossroads recently. I had to move house. That phrase itself can be troublesome. The decent reader will know immediately that it means changing from one house into another or – to be even more explicit – shifting the furniture. The reasons for having to do this are innumerable. It might be a natural growth in the family, the terrible smell from some putrescence in the garden next door, or an all-out attempt to shift the wife's mother, who came for a fortnight in 1926.

But changing house is not as easy as it looks, if it ever looked easy. Most of us do not know how complicated being born frequently is because we don't remember the occurrence. But nobody who has changed house is likely to forget it. I write this 'at home', i.e., the change has not yet been made. But the bruises of the 'softening up' artillery barrage are still very keenly felt. I am plain scared. The day takes on the sombre guise of *Der Tag*. Translating a simple term into German seems to give it a sinister edge.

It is only on moving house that a man realises the unbelievable assortment of stuff with which he has surrounded himself in – say – ten years. Start, say, with old letters. They should have been torn up many years ago, of course, but they are still there, hoarded and yellowing. The householder cannot make out who wrote them and about what. What is the meaning of the postcard which is headed *warning* in indigo ink with the message *If it happens again action will be taken*?

Under the stairs in a rusty biscuit tin is a lady's full length ball dress probably fashionable early in the reign of Victoria. Why is it there and who put it there? It couldn't be the property of your wife because she had not been born when it was in vogue and anyway would not be seen dead in such a ludicrous invention. For that matter, what is the front assembly of a child's Edwardian tricycle doing under your bed? Who put *that* there?

Brain Washing

The removal merchants are quite alive to the speculative nature of their trade and the unpredictable character of their customers. You are a sober, prudent individual and you go to one of them to get an estimate of cost of house removal. Jaunty as your step may be going in, you feel very much in need of an ambulance coming out – as I did. I set out initially to give the reader a word-by-word account of my interview but now find I cannot: it would be too harrowing. But let me just lift the hem. I am shown into a small room in which is seated at a desk a ruffianly-looking Gauleiter who does not look at me but barks out a demand for my name and address. I sit on a chair facing him, for there is no other. The dialogue starts like this:

'Moving? I see. Scaling things down, ah? Lost the job, I suppose?'

'I didn't lose any job.'

'I have them in here every day. Drink. The number of decent men destroyed by drink is terrible. It is drink, drink, drink, night and day. Home, family and religion – all is ignored. Just drink and then more drink.'

'If you refer to intoxicants, I may say I never touch them.'

He looked up at me for the first time and frowned.

'But there's just one thing worse than drink,' he rasped. *'Women!'*

'I have been happily married,' I managed to croak, 'for twenty-five years.'

'I have them in here every day. And the married men are the worst. Home, faith, fatherland – all gone down the Swanee to fly after some ugly strap of a farmer's daughter.'

'I happen to be married to a farmer's daughter and she is not an ugly strap.'

'And that's another thing. The children are neglected. Never get a decent hot meal, dressed in rags and out all day robbing orchards. A law unto themselves. And you call this a Christian country.'

'I didn't call this country anything.'

'And then you have every spare penny spent on those dirty papers they send over from London.'

I can't go on – not this week, anyhow. In five minutes I had completely forgotten the object of my call, which was to get a quotation for the removal of furniture. I found myself making abject confessions on small but rather personal matters such as occasionally sleeping in my shirt on particularly cold nights in winter. I cannot remember whether at some stage I broke down and cried. Certainly I was terrified. The ogre opposite me seemed Evil incarnate. I will see if I am strong enough this day week to take up again the shattered thread of my narrative. Right now I am going out to have a small whiskey.

That business about moving house

I presume this week to lay to my heart this flattering unction that the reader who looks at this also saw what I said last week about the havoc and horror of 'moving house'. I promised to continue the grim record. Today I make the attempt. I write this 'at home'. Those gaunt words may possibly convey what I mean. I have not yet been railroaded. I am still at home, but in a very quaking one. How soon will the ceiling come down?

The ogre whom I had met in his own office had said that before an estimate could be given, an inspection would be necessary. At the time I thought this reasonable enough. After all, if somebody has to shift something, surely that somebody is entitled to a preview of the stuff to be shifted?

The Inspector Cometh

I was in a state of terror. Every knock at the door gave me fresh spasms.

Eventually, the worst happened. Himself was on the doorstep. I had quite forgotten about this sinister term 'Inspection' but was soon to learn its true meaning. He was to auction stuff, therefore wanted to know what the stuff was. The true meaning of the word was *The Great Snoop*, the derogation of myself personally and the undisguised implication that my property was rubbish.

I opened the door myself. He stepped into the hall and, to my alarm, started to take off coat and hat. This clearly meant he was going to stay for a while if not, indeed, for a whole weekend. My wife had often reproached me for my bad companions and dissolute pals. What would she make of this situation when she returned from her morning shopping? It boded ill for me.

'I'll just stick this stuff,' he said, fingering his outer vestments, 'on the rack.'

The thing I have in my hall is what is commonly called a hall-stand. It is a sort of family heirloom, made of mahogany and at least a hundred years old. At least technically it is an antique and may be of great value. I would be surprised but not quite flabbergasted if a diligent search of its interior revealed the inscription 'A. Stradivarius fecit' carefully concealed. Yet this gorilla called it a rack!

'I hope you're not going to take this up,' he said, stamping on the floor of my hall, 'it's always better to keep the floor covered when you're selling. Woodworm, you know. Buyers are cuter than you think.'

It was perfectly good linoleum, bought not two years before. I just gaped. He was already in the main living-room off the hall.

'Well, good heavens,' he said as if stunned, '– what is that?'

'You mean with the four legs?'

'Yes, just there in the centre.'

'It is supposed to be a table.'

He laughed coarsely and made an entry in a small dirty notebook he had produced. 'We might even call it an *objet d'art* at that,' he remarked. 'The legs is all bawways. But we could throw it in with something worth flogging. People count every half crown these days, you know.'

He sat down on a chair but got up very suddenly and led the way into the next apartment, which I like to call the drawing-room. I'll admit it's a bit old-fashioned and I never really liked the faded yellow wallpaper. But the armchairs, in heavy brocade, were attractive in their own way and the great gilt mirror over the mantelpiece was truly a work of art, the frame having been designed by some unknown Italian master. My inspector paused on the threshold as if startled.

'I suppose,' he said, leering, 'that you will be looking for a small fortune for the hearthrug? Or should we call it a bit of fancy carpet?'

I followed his pointing finger.

'You mean at the fireplace? That is not a hearthrug and is not for sale. That is Annie. Annie is a sheepdog. That clear?'

In the Bedroom

One humiliation followed another. Perhaps the worst occurred in my bedroom.

'What's this?' he asked. 'A pantry?'

'It is not a pantry,' I said acidly.

'Another table,' he said without heeding my tone, 'Why on earth have you a soiled blanket on it?'

'You mean that article by the window. It has four legs but it is not a table.'

'Well what is it if I'm not asking you to spill a secret?'

'It's my bed.'

'Mean to say you sleep in that? Well, well . . .'

And so it went on. He called my inlaid walnut wardrobe 'the press'. It was just one litany of insult. When about to take his merciful departure, he said this:

'I'll ask Kelly to come and have a look and give us a price. But I'll tell you a funny thing about shifting furniture.'

'What?' I asked, frankly dismayed. He put on an oracular frown.

'It costs just the same,' he intoned, 'to shift good stuff as junk. Sometimes it costs more because rubbish often collapses when it's moved. The removal man has to allow for that. Everything here is riddled with wood-worm. But the men who deal in this sort of trade are cute enough. I know one character that takes on decorating jobs, hanging paper and all that. He has one iron rule. In an old place like this, he will paper the whole place for you but he'll put the new paper on top of the old. Know why?'

'I do not.'

'If you were to take the paper off the walls of an ancient joint like this, the walls might collapse. The paper holds the house together. Do you follow?'

I showed him out. What else could I do? Then I nearly passed out.

The forgetting of eaten bread

In the last year or so I have come to suspect that I am possessed of a great blessing which will bring me great solace, happiness, and the boon of the eternal ever-new; or else that I am labouring under a terrible curse, a sort of cerebral derangement that sooner or later is bound to get me into serious trouble.

The other night I was at my bookshelves looking for a certain volume and was surprised to see there *Lady Gregory's Journals, 1916–1930,* edited by Lennox Robinson. Where had this come from? I opened it at page 96 – the secret page on which I write my name to catch out borrowers and book-sharks – and my signature was there all right. The book was mine. I opened it here and there and found nothing I could recollect as having seen before. Eventually I sat down and read the whole thing, and every bit of it was new. Yet I MUST have read it before. You see my dilemma? I seem to have the gift of totally forgetting in a very short time everything I read. This miraculously renews my library every year or so.

It was not an old book – first published 1946 by Putnam. 'Old book'? What am I talking about? Beside it on the shelf were two others. One was Xenophontos Kurou Paideias – Biblia Okto, published in London in 1765; among the printers was T. Caslon, a member of the family of great typefounders after whom the Caslon fount is still named. Greek text impeccable, all footnotes and comment in faultless Latin; probably a valuable volume. The other book was a collection of poems by Alfred Tennyson, published in 1842. Nothing remarkable in that, perhaps, except for the inscription on the title page in spidery faded writing: 'William R. Hamilton, Observatory'. Imagine the great inventor of quaternions wallowing in Tennyson!

Augusta Regina

It is a fascinating book, though the *Journals* are necessarily severely abridged. Augusta Perrse was born in 1852 at Roxboro', Co. Galway, and strictly of the old landlord class, her father at one time owning over 4,000 acres. In 1880 she married Sir William Gregory, an MP, of nearby Coole Park. He died in 1892 but she had one son, Robert, who was killed in the 1914 war. Sir Hugh Lane was her nephew and the recent tortuous part-return of the Lane pictures has brought Lady Gregory's memory back to many people, for those pictures were one of the great worries and preoccupations of her life.

The urge to keep a diary is a curious one, and can even be dangerous. What a to-do there has been over those Casement diaries! But in those 42 typewritten volumes of *Lady Gregory's Journal*, she has left a vivid portrait of herself, her friends and contemporaries, and her times. She wrote well and had an amazing memory right to her death at the age of 80 in 1932.

On her husband's death she naturally took over Coole Park and, although never quite severing her ancient landlord allegiance, she took an extraordinary and kindly interest in the local people, was interested in all flower and plant life, became deeply engrossed in folklore and local customs, in due course came like her neighbour Edward Martyn to support avidly the Gaelic League and virtually became a sort of upper-class separatist and Republican, though her sympathies here lay more in the cultural sphere.

Most people are aware of the main compartments of her career: her life-long friendship with W. B. Yeats; the Abbey Theatre, her tasks there in both management and playwriting; the Lane pictures; and her experiences in both the Black-and-Tan terror and the Civil war, followed by the slow establishment of the Free State. Her day-to-day account of those last-named episodes is extraordinarily impressive and vivid, for such an account has an immediacy that any formal history written long in arrear must lack. Her narrative of Black-and-Tan terrorism – the murders, beatings, burnings, robberies and looting – would startle those younger people whose personal memory does not embrace that terrible era. Her own position in remote Coole required courage, for her interest in native things and people was not healthy when demented Black and Tans were at large and unused to making fine distinctions; but of personal courage it is clear that she had any amount.

The Abbey Theatre

The Abbey, its genesis and growth, was the focus of her life and personality, and many people will be absorbed by the first timid appearance and the development and triumph of the well-loved players so many of whom are now dead – Sally Allgood, F. J. McCormick, Michael Dolan, Arthur Sinclair, Will Shields, and many more. Another different if complementary panorama is presented in the comings and goings of the many new playwrights the Abbey brought forth; money was always tight, there were constant rows and bickerings and nearly everybody concerned – players and playwrights alike – had to have their first reliance on ordinary modest jobs by day. Normal pay for a top actor was for many years of the order of £4 a week, and these were people who created a new theatre and a new mode of acting. Barry Fitzgerald was in late middle age before he could dare to throw up a modest job in the civil service. Yeats himself was, of course, a great inspiration to all but he was by no means a man of affairs and often caused annoyance and irritation.

Sean O'Casey was the centre of the greatest upheaval. After the great success of *Juno* had established him, *The Plough and the Stars* led to disorders and near-riots very reminiscent of Synge's *Playboy* opening. But when the Abbey Board rejected the *Silver Tassie*, the row and recriminations were immense and led to O'Casey's self-imposed exile. Yet nobody could quarrel with Lady Gregory herself, not even O'Casey.

Some People

There are many intimate little portraits of famous people who were Lady Gregory's friends – Bernard Shaw, Sir Horace Plunkett, Lady Ardilaun, Gogarty, A. E. Martyn, George Moore, James Stephens and many others. It is perhaps no coincidence that they were all not only talented but also very decent people, for it is impossible to imagine Augusta permitting herself to associate with wrong types. She had a sense of humour, too, and is quite funny about the take-over of the Vice-regal Lodge, the arrival of Tim Healy and the succession in due time of the MacNeills.

I never met Lady Gregory but some six or seven years ago I accompanied Michael Scott, the architect, to Coole; he had been retained to design a plaque for Yeats's Norman Tower at Ballylee, hard by. We visited Coole itself, now in the hands of the Land Commission. The wooded approach drive is magnificent but of Lady Gregory's beloved mansion not one trace remains.

Some big blunders in literature

The father of Benjamin D'Israeli, later to become the Earl of Beaconsfield, was Isaac D'Israeli, with the life-span of 1766–1848. He was a writer and much interested in a subject he called literary history; his reading was vast, his gift for languages exceptional, and his erudition well-founded and deep. Apart from some novels and poems, his best-known work was *Curiosities of Literature* which was issued in several parts between 1791 and 1834: it is a veritable treasure-home of what is odd, comic and fascinating.

On a book-barrow I have come on one of the volumes of some 550 pages published in 1839 and today I think I could do worse than purloin some of the facts he has collected under the title of *Literary Blunders*. At least I will not be infringing his copyright.

Credulous Readers

The cynicism and doubts of our own age did not exist in Isaac's day. When Dante's *Inferno* was published it was widely accepted as a true narrative of the poet's descent into hell. Similarly when Sir Thomas More's *Utopia* appeared, nearly everybody believed that this visionary republic really existed, thought the book was genuine history and a movement was set on foot to send missionaries there to convert so wise a people to Christianity.

A certain clownish writer named Dr Campbell published an ingenious work named *Hermippus Redivuvus* which pretended to be a treatise on hermetic philosophy and universal medicine. So well did he maintain his portentous style, that several educated people were taken in.

He argued that human life could be prolonged by inhaling the breath of young women. Another physician who had himself written learnedly on health matters, eagerly accepted this new doctrine to the extent of taking lodgings in a ladies' boarding school so that he could have the students' breath in abundant supply, and many other people took similar steps.

A commentator named Fabiani, quoting a French account of travels in Italy, mistook for the name of the author these words he found at end of title-page *Enrichi de deux Listes* (or 'Enriched with two lists'). He wrote: 'That Mr Enriched with two lists has not failed to do justice to Ciampini' – a district he had visited.

The Unperceiving Clergy

Our anecdotal archivist Isaac, whose family were Jews from Venice, quite often found part of his fun in the writings and doings of ministers of the Christian Church. There is however no rancour in his discoveries. Some of the monks of yesteryear were rather ignorant and one of Isaac's stories concerns a legal row a certain pastor had with his parishioners concerning the responsibility for paying the cost of paving the church. The priest went to the reputed writings of St Peter and quoted the phrase *Paveant illi, non paveam ego.* He thought this meant 'They are to pave the church, not I.' In fact the Latin verb *paveo* means 'I am trembling from terror' and has nothing whatever to do with paving.

Collie Cibber wrote a play he called *Love's Last Shift.* It was very popular and in due course translated into French. The translator named it *La Dernière Chemise de l'Amour.*

The valued Latin writer Petronius was for many centuries famed (or notorious) for the fact that his surviving writings were fragmentary. The world of learning was startled when a professor in Lübeck got a letter from another in Bologna saying, 'We have *an entire Petronius here*; I saw it with my own eyes.' The Lübeck man hastened immediately to Bologna, sought out his correspondent and asked to be shown 'the entire petronius'. He was conducted to a church and shown the body of St Petronius.

Another writer, translating a treatise on Judaism from Latin to French, rendered *Omnis bonus liber est* by 'Tout livre est bon', a remark that would no doubt enrage our own censorship board.

Tom Brown's Guesswork

Still another writer named Tom Brown whom at the moment I cannot identify was translating a composition named *Circe*, presumably in German, and came upon the word *Starne*, the meaning of which he was not sure about. Apparently relying on the sound of the word, he translated it 'stares'. But a later translator went to the trouble of making sure what *Starne* meant and found it was red-legged partridges!

These are merely samples from Isaac D'Israeli's essay on literary blunders but gives some idea of his tireless search for absurdity. Another day I hope to summarise his comment on other subjects, for there was apparently no limit to his choice of matters for discourse. It is a pity to find nowadays that he is out of print and quite unknown to nearly everybody.

Oh, dear me! more holidays!

I am sure everybody knows the original link between holiday and holy day. A good few centuries before now, important Church holidays were preceded by a period of light-heartedness on the part of the faithful. It is true that the hearts got lighter than they had any right to, and the situation looks the more odd when one reflects that those customs arose a long time before anybody dreamt of conceding the working classes anything in the way of real 'time off'.

Not so much in Britain – and certainly not in poor Ireland – the excesses of the people on the continent in medieval times just when an important religious event was in the offing were considerable indeed, and not infrequently seriously worried the local Prince or Landgrave. Perhaps the root of the worry was not so much that they were drinking or dancing too much, or behaving riotously, but simply that they were not doing any work. What about the sowing of the harvest, the vines, or the mere mending of shoes? But the Church itself did not condemn such procedures out of hand, and over the centuries some system of accommodation was found.

This age of ours should not be regarded, as too readily it is, as the one which invented appeasement. In what I have said above I indicate where most of us got what we call our holidays, and how this most suspicious thing started at all. Holidays in the ordinary sense are a turbulence, a disturbance, an abomination and a terrifying nuisance.

The Awful Seaside

I suppose we all have our recollections of our earlier holidays, all bristling with horror. What about being

25

packed off as toddlers to stay with the aunt for six weeks? That stern lady who made custard every day and who otherwise thought the staff of life was porridge? You remember those tyrannical obsessions about washing necks, going to bed early, and being respectful? These procedures can have a disastrous consequence; now myself approaching middle age, I think I can truthfully say that I have not properly washed my neck since 1931.

But the most critical disaster was surely the discovery about a century ago of the sea by the land-bound British. They found the sea was very good for you, not in its ancient sense as an occasion of empire and world conquest but as something to get into on mild strands and let it cover you up to the oxters and maybe higher. The 'resorts' then came to the fore, the 'bathing machines', the sand, the buckets, the unbelievable seaside lodgings and ultimately the pier with its band, phoney negroes, ice cream, and that most marvellous of all atrocities – Sundays when absolutely nothing was permitted.

Naturally Ireland was slow in following this cross-channel opulence of expansion to the letter, yet not a few good men and true still alive here are innocent of a youth which did not have some of that terrifying quality. Skerries, for instance. I have carried around in my juvenile socks more of the sand of that place than would rebuild the Four Courts, again and again I have fallen on the weedy slime of its rocks to the extent of splitting my sconce, and once spent two months every summer in a house which, though two-storeyed, slated and fine, had no running water or sewerage. (To be just, I think arrangements are a bit better now.)

Do people still go in for this lunacy? Well, I suppose they do. But why? That's a big question.

Some New Ideas

Yet all is not bleakness. I think the main boon for a person going away for a while is to make it crystal-clear to himself and all others that he is not going on his holidays. The person who uses that horrible phrase is bunched. A business-trip, perhaps? To Istanbul?

I do think the seaside holiday is largely discredited. But take care that something worse does not take its place, for something far worse nearly happened to my good self just before Easter. Two chaps I know were good enough to ask me whether I would care to join them on three or four days away from it all? The idea sounded good but I was suspicious. A quick trip by air to Tunis? Nice enough, but surely expensive; even a bit dangerous, perhaps, with all those gun-happy characters in Morocco. I gave a tentative three cheers but modestly asked where they were going. Oh, Galway – Kerry, maybe. Fine – but how?

By Caravan!

I did not back down on the spot. This, I said, was a new thing and terribly interesting. I would see them, I explained, the following night for a further talk. And so I did, bringing a loose but commodious waterproof bag reasonably filled for the novel trip the day after. I was asked what was in it? Just a few essentials, I explained – a few clean shirts, pyjamas, change of pants and jackets, soap, shaving gear, a few towels, a raincoat, some elementary medical stores, and a bottle of whiskey.

I can only report that the row was appalling. Did I think I was going on safari to darkest Africa? Who did I think I was? What did I mean by shaving? Surely I knew what it was for a few fellows to knock about together for a few days in the land of their birth? Towels?

I didn't know much about a few fellows knocking about a few days – and don't. I didn't go. But I brought that whiskey safely home.

Manners also maketh the boy

My business, varied and mysterious as some may judge it, frequently brings me to Dublin city and entails bus trips about the suburbs. I have encountered one startling thing so often in the early afternoon and in different localities that I think I might mention it here.

The bus is nearly empty and I am on the top deck, peaceably trying to read a paper. It pulls up at a stop and presently all bedlam breaks out. Shouts and shrieks fill the air and the vehicle shudders as it is assailed apparently by a horde of redskins. There is a clattering on the stairs and suddenly the whole upper saloon is filled with an inundation of bawling schoolboys aged, I should say, between 8 and 12.

Nearly all of them carry a sort of toffee apple on a stick which is brandished indiscriminately between sucks, on one occasion smearing the clothes of my innocent self. The noise is deafening and fights start here and there. They kneel and stand on the seats. The last time this happened to me, the company had an important notice about time-table changes pasted to the curved bulkhead above the windows but one corner of the notice was loose and detached. One lad stood on the seat, got a hold of this corner and methodically began to tear the notice down.

The reader must not think I am censuring the natural exuberance of youth and, in case it should matter, the boys were nearly all well dressed and did not look as if they attended the conventional national school. They were brats. Do they behave like this in the schoolroom? If they do, teaching some juniors must be a greater martyrdom than is commonly supposed, though it would be quite unfair to expect teachers single-handed to try to eradicate this mode of conduct. That is primarily the duty of the parents. And the prognosis could be grim enough. I am afraid that some at least of those characters are embryo teddy-boys.

Of Yesterday

I am sure some readers may have heard of a little book entitled *The Accomplished Gentleman or Principles of Politeness and of Knowing the World* by Philip Stanhope, Earl of Chesterfield. My own copy is published by James Duffy of Dublin and dated 1844.

I will grant that parts of this treatise are funny and the mere date alone countermands many of the principles he lays down, for even manners have some dependence on contemporary fashion and custom. All the same much of what he teaches could with great benefit be absorbed by those schoolboys, for he is addressing 'every young gentleman'.

He praises modesty and reprobates all insolence, boasting, shouting and extravagant behaviour, and strongly condemns lying, which he discerns as originating in vanity and cowardice. He considers the essence of good breeding is absence of rudeness and ruffianly self-assertion. At table the awkward fellow is easy to discern. 'He sets himself upon the edge of the chair, at so great a distance from the table, that he frequently drops his meat between his plate and his mouth; he holds his knife, fork and spoon differently from other people; eats with his knife, to the manifest danger of his mouth; picks his teeth with his fork, rakes his mouth with his finger, and puts his spoon, which has been in his mouth a dozen times, into the dish again. If he is to carve, he cannot hit the joint, but in labouring to cut through the bone, splashes the sauce over everybody's clothes. He generally daubs himself all over, his elbow is in the next person's plate, and he is up to his knuckles in soup and grease.'

In that much I think Lord Chesterfield was mostly

concerned with etiquette, and it was not in etiquette that I found those schoolboys so deficient.

Dress and Laughter

One of the subjects on which his lordship's advice is obsolete is that of dress. Let me quote again:

'There are few young fellows but what display some character or other in this shape. Some would be thought fearless and brave: these wear a black cravat, a short coat and waistcoat, an uncommon long sword hanging to the knees, a large hat fiercely cocked, and are flash all over. Others affect to be country squires; these will go about in buckskin breeches, brown frocks, and a great oaken cudgel in their hands, slouched hats, with their hair undressed, and tucked up under them, to an enormous size...'

I complained of wanton noise in the bus. He holds that loud and frequent laughter is sure evidence of a weak mind and quite inexcusable if the pretext for it is that when another man is about to sit down, you pull the chair away so that he falls on the floor. Loose language, mispronounced language and even bad language 'must be avoided, if you would not be supposed to have kept company with footmen and housemaids'.

His lordship undoubtedly has some stern attitudes. He advises against playing cards or drinking. Excess in drink is the mark of the blackguard, though moderate drinking when unavoidable (e.g. a toast at a wedding) is permitted. But suppose playing cards is a social duty. A person in such a spot 'will not be seen at cribbage, all-fours, or putt'. Seemliness at games is also important and those schoolboys might note that a wellbred person 'will not be seen at skittles, football, leap-frog, cricket . . .' If music be your interest, be careful here again. 'Piping or fiddling at a concert is degrading to a man of fashion. If you love music, hear it; pay fiddlers to play for you, but never fiddle yourself. It makes a gentleman appear frivolous and contemptible.'

There are many other matters I may mention another day but perhaps special school buses and not Chesterfield are the real remedy for my own problem.

Bringing back the Gaelic tongue

Some stir has been caused by the turning down of a motion at a recent meeting of the Dublin Corporation. The motion was that a former resolution be rescinded and that for the future the title of all new roads on Corporation estates should be put up bilingually, not in Irish only as heretofore. Many people had complained that they did not know Irish and had the greatest difficulty in finding given addresses.

Passers-by whom they stopped could not help much and other people complained that although they had no trouble in making their way home, they could not say where they lived – postally. One man wrote sarcastically to the papers saying that he fully appreciated the Corporation's attitude, that those who objected were shoneens, but that the Corporation should now carry on its deliberations in Irish only and that the minutes and records should be kept only in that language.

Stupid Mistakes

The curiosity is that Corporation name-plates bristle with stupid mistakes in the Irish, and the plates are expensive enamel or cast-iron affairs incapable of amendment. I once had a list of them, now long mislaid, but I clearly remember one. In the old days a saintly man was saying his matins on the banks of the Dodder and was attacked by a gang of louts, who fired his holy book into the river. Promptly a badger appeared with the book in his mouth and restored it to the saint and soon at this spot a church was built. It was called Domhnach Broc, church of the badger, or Donnybrook. Several Corporation plates in the area give the Irish name for Donnybrook as Domhnach Broch.

There is no such word as Broch.

A similar mess is made all over Dublin and the whole country in the matter of putting up the Irish names of sub-post offices. It is a rarity to see a wholly correct inscription.

The Long Journey

All the trouble, agitation and work to revive the use of the Irish language is about 100 years old. In 1860 there were over a million native speakers in the country, many communities as far east as Tipperary and Roscommon, and at Omagh and Antrim. I do not suppose that there are 200,000 left who speak Irish 'from the cradle'.

It is impossible to assess the extent or value of teaching Irish in all the schools since the foundation of the State but it is a fair guess that the language learnt, even well learnt, is not true Irish. Scarcely ever anywhere is an acquired tongue the true thing and that holds even where a transposed person is in an environment where nothing but the other tongue is spoken. In fact, as languages go, Irish is a very difficult language, totally alien to the European mould.

A Trinity Man

I happen to have a formidable library of literature relating to the revival, including many bound volumes of the *Claidheamh Soluis* and the earlier Gaelic Journal, issued by the Gaelic Union. In 1886, when the President of the latter body was The Right Hon. the O'Connor Don and the Patron The Most Rev. Dr Croke, Archbishop of Cashel, I am ever delighted to note the particulars of a Trinity man who was on the Council. Here is the name as it appears on the official list:

'Rev. Samuel Haughton, MD, FRS, FGS, SFTCD,

DCL (Oxon), PRIA, MA, LLD, F K & QCPI, FGRSI.'

It is nice to know that so learned a man did not despise the Irish tongue.

I think the first formal body dedicated to reviving Irish was the Ossianic Society – one omits, of course, the Royal Irish Academy, founded in 1782. Next came the Society for the Preservation of the Irish Language, then the Gaelic Union and in 1897 the Gaelic League. After that, cumanns and clubs were ten a penny.

Do We Know Much?

Has there been any genuine progress? I cannot truly say but don't believe the man who tells you he doesn't know a word of Irish. It isn't true.

The same man may take a dander down the *boreen*, raising his *cawb* to the *soggarth shebeen* to have several *glawsheens* of *usquebaugh* in his *cruiskeen lawn*. When he has become a bit unsteady on his *croobs*, he will try to give a *pogue* to the *benatee*, whether she is *colleen dhas*, a *shan van vocht*, a *banshee*, or a *streel*, calling her his *mavourneen*. He will become talkative and begin discussing the market for *bonavs* with sundry other *omadhauns, shanachies, ownshucks, cawbogues, loodera-mauns, spalpeens* and even *leprechauns*, his *doodeen* stuck in his *gob*. After ordering a pound of *drisheen* and a pound of *croobeens* to bring to *céili* he is going to, he will call for a *duckandurus* and *fooster* about, proposing a drunken *sláinte* to all and trying to *grig* the son of the house by calling him a *sleeveen*. Tottering home leaning on his *slane* like a bemused *pooka*, he will stop to talk to a *gossoon* about *pinkeens*. A *garda* will bring him the rest of the way. He will be met by his wife and it won't be 100,000 *fawlthah* she will put before him.

Sure we're all practically native speakers.

Men and women of the roads

It seems that many people, puzzled and fed up with almost daily confrontation with the prospect of cosmic crisis and catastrophe, turn almost with relief to problems which are much nearer home and of considerably lesser gravity.

Just now tinkers have become a subject of pretty widespread concern and interest but the public attitude to them has been far from uniform. Some ten days ago it was reported that near Mullingar a herd of about 20 donkeys had broken into a holding, devoured everything green in sight, including a large plot of cabbages, and were then seen departing 'in a southerly direction'. They were said to belong to tinkers encamped nearby, and there can be little doubt as to the feelings of the ruined farmer.

Only a few days ago while waiting for a bus by the side of what is reputedly the most heavily-trafficked and dangerous road in Ireland, I saw a large mare with a little foal ambling along the centre of the thoroughfare. They were unperturbed by swerves and the shriek of brakes until a grassy bank attracted them. They could have been killed or have caused the death of a whole carful of people, though grazing their animals on the verges of public roads, with no watch or control over them, has been the settled, long-standing practice of gypsies – that is, when they cannot get them into the fields of farmers. Yet at several public discussions on the subject (one in the Dáil) several speakers took the side of the tinkers and argued that they should be persuaded to settle down in houses provided by local authorities and that they were very decent romantic folk.

Unthinkable Facts

The prominence the subject has attained seems to indicate that tinkers are increasing in number, and I have heard the total genuine tinker population of the whole country estimated at 6,500. Is this a social trend, provoked by rocketing rates and taxes? Hard to say but there is no denying that tinkers in their way of life can be not only a nuisance but a danger.

With their livestock they cause damage to property and traffic danger.

Many of them steal and send their womenfolk begging, usually armed with an ailing child.

Their sanitation arrangements are either nil or of the most primitive kind, and thus menace the public health.

Their children, usually very numerous, do not go to school and grow up to be little savages.

A tinkers' camp is too often the centre of mêlées or other disorders.

Their moral code is deplorable.

It is clear from the above that several of their practices are *prima facie* unlawful but for some reason not obvious, the Guards will take no action unless a specific complaint is made to them in respect of a particular occurrence.

An advocate for the defence may blandly inquire what about the new type of tinker or nomad who is ever more frequently to be encountered – the kind who hauls a luxurious caravan behind a powerful motor car? It is a fallacious comparison. The new wayfarers are merely on a holiday, seek the permission of landowners when camping and do not have livestock, while in several spots in the country caravan sites, fully equipped with sanitation and drinking water, are being provided for a small charge. The genuine tinker spends his whole life moving about in those rickety vans of which few people have ever seen the inside. It must be an awful life in the middle of a real Irish winter.

Who Are They?

Many people profess to make a sharp distinction between the gypsy and the tinker; the latter so-called because he repairs tin vessels while the former is a gaudy, light-hearted romany, swarthy with flashing eyes, bedecked with ear-rings and sashes, fond of music and playing the fiddle. I fear this distinction does not exist and probably originated in the cinema. The word gypsy is properly Egyptian, from whence those nomads came to Europe. The French call him a *Bohémien* and the Germans a *Zigeuner*, and philologists argue that 'tinker' is an attempt to render the latter sound into English. The womenfolk have always been noted, though not so much in this country, for their pretences (or skill) at fortune-telling. It is true that the men often practised metalwork and were good at that craft but it was usually in copper, not tin.

The clans have never been trusted. Henry VIII issued several severe edicts against them and in 1611 three were hanged at Edinburgh 'for abyding within the kingdome, they being Egiptienis' and in 1636 the Egyptians were ordered 'the men to hangied and the weomen to be drowned, and suche of the weomen as hes children to be scourgit throw the burg and burnt in the cheeks.'

In what we call their family life tinkers in Ireland seem to behave conventionally enough, though elsewhere polygamy and incest are practised and even cannibalism has been alleged.

Two oddities arise: first, in a world where the displaced person has become a large and tragic problem, here we have people who have voluntarily displaced themselves and seem to enjoy that status. Second, good citizens who pay taxes and live in houses but who are thought to have committed certain and various offences are brought before the court on a charge of vagrancy.

Some other day we may consider the tramp. He is a very different man.

The great perils of being nursed

It is common enough knowledge that doctors are a closely enough knit body; they do not speak out of turn, quarrel with each other publicly or make any comment that might suggest that all is not as it might be with the care of the sick.

One was much surprised, therefore, at some outspoken remarks made a few weeks ago by Dr Brian Pringle at the annual meeting of Monkstown Hospital, Dublin. He mentioned many matters which required to be attended to in the management of hospitals so far as the patients were concerned. Presumably he was referring to Dublin hospitals but his remarks may have a country-wide application. As a former patient (broken leg) perhaps I may amplify and supplement what he said. Sick people are quite defenceless and it is sad to say that every advantage is often taken of this condition.

Peep O'Day

Nearly all the general hospitals in Dublin are structurally not much better than slums; the buildings are over two centuries old, many unsuitable and dangerous, and most without any proper fire escape system. Through some disastrous breakdown initially of the Hospitals' Commission (which surveys hospital needs and recommends grants from the Sweepstake Funds) hardly any significant capital works were provided for over the years for the Dublin area. The new National Maternity Hospital at Holles Street was rebuilt, for the old one was positively tottering, and a big new fever hospital has been provided; but these are specialised services.

Dr Pringle mentioned the universal practice of rousing patients, even in mid-winter, at the unearthly hour of 6 a.m., compelling them to wash and shave, have beds made and then try to face a breakfast which I personally always found poor and usually cold. The whole practice is barbarous and must be injurious.

The doctor also mentioned the strain caused by noise. He may have meant internal work noises or the clatter of traffic from without but there is another form of noise that could almost lead to the loss of reason. A modern peril is radiation sickness but what I mean here is radio sickness. You are in a ward with, say, twelve other sufferers. One of them has a radio which he keeps turned on full blast all day. But another also has a radio and exercises the same 'right', though not necessarily interested in the same station. The incessant din is excruciating and nothing is done about it. Occasionally a table with crucifix is set up at a bed, a clear enough sign that somebody is about to receive the Last Rites. No notice of this is taken, and I have honestly seen a poor man die to the strains of the Blue Danube.

The meals seem to be improvised and certainly cannot come from a modern kitchen designed for mass catering. The meat used is invariably low-grade mutton, usually boiled or stewed. A tough neighbour of my own told me he had got far better fare in Mountjoy Prison where, indeed, the ration for everybody includes five cigarettes per day.

Fading Eyesight

A personal experience of my own may be worth recounting. Treatment for a broken leg usually entails having the whole limb impaled in plaster and a bar driven through the heel; from this bar wires are fixed to run over pulleys at the bottom of the bed and carrying heavy weights, the idea being to prevent the limb contracting when the break begins to knit. It all means that the poor patient must lie immovably on the flat of his back for several months, quite helpless.

The ward which found me in this position in mid-winter was an enormously lofty apartment, with beds lining the walls latterly on each side. Lighting was provided by a series of powerful lamps suspended from the centre of the ceiling. These lamps began to blaze at about 4.30 in the evening. Reading was, of course, out of the question since any book or paper would be in complete shadow. A patient unable to turn on his side had no alternative but to lie staring at this light. I complained to a matron that I thought this situation would cause me eventually to lose my eyesight, that I was having attacks of double-vision and that my eyes were already red and smarting. I was told for goodness sake to have sense and not be talking nonsense. My own resource came to the rescue. I bade a visitor speed off to the shops and get me the sort of green eye-shade one sees at the Central Court at Wimbledon. I was proud of this brainwave and prouder still when I saw that everybody else in the ward had one a few days after.

It is not easy to know in what quarter to assign the blame for such outrageous things. The doctor or nursing staff can scarcely be blamed, for their own work must be rendered the more difficult thereby. Most hospitals of the kind termed 'voluntary' are under the direction of a board, mostly of charitable laymen. I am not aware that they ever visit the wards and see how the house is run.

I cannot say what conditions are like in Laois but I fear that being a patient in any hospital in Ireland calls for two things – holy resignation and an iron constitution.

The ancient game of name-calling

Provided big changes occur gradually, they are hardly noticed. There is no outcry about getting rheumatic, grey and old because those conditions assert themselves almost imperceptibly. In the days of my youth when living near Tullamore, I was well used to seeing farmers coming home in the evening from the fair, unconscious from drink in the bottom of a donkey-cart. That sagacious animal, keeping to his own side of the road, brought the boss safely home.

At that time one of the nastiest crimes of today had not been invented. I mean drunken driving. And within the last ten years or so, the whole routine of living socially has been drastically altered by television. Similarly, people slowly begin to forget one language and speak another. This process of change is endemic, ageless and unavoidable. Physiologists claim that the physical structure of a human being is wholly renewed every seven years and it is on record that one man tried to get out of paying back an old debt because it was somebody else, not himself, who had contracted the debt some eight years before.

New electronic aids have rendered old-fashioned and obsolete the system of learning things (which simply have to be remembered) by heart. That was the way most of us learnt which prepositions in Latin take the dative and ablative case, learnt the alphabet and our prayers. Another aid to memory was the plan of committing information to verse.

Forgotten Man

I think I have already remarked here on the extra-ordinary fact that there is no memoir or biography in existence of John O'Donovan, the great Gaelic scholar of the last century; worse, his books are long out of print and circulation and it is only in one or two central libraries that one can consult, say, his edition of the Annals of the Four Masters. In Duffy's attractive monthly magazine, the *Hibernian Sixpenny Magazine* for May 1862, there is a review of O'Donovan's edition of *Topographical Poems*, being the work of two scribes named O Dubhagáin (died 1372) and O hUidhrin (died 1420). Their compilations deal with the location territorially of well-known ancient Irish families and are more a genealogical than a topographical record. The edition shows O'Donovan as a smart enough detective in finding out who people with strange and obviously foreign names really were after the great changes in the country following the Anglo-Norman invasion. Some of the patronymics were compulsorily conferred. In 1465 Edward IV decreed that every Irishman living in the Pale should take an English surname or, to quote the exact words, 'shall take to him an English surname of one town, as Sutton, Chester, Trym, Skyrne, Corke, Kinsale; or colour, as White, Blacke, Browne; or art or science, as Smith or Carpenter; or office, as Cooke, Butler.'

This command was widely carried out, a family named Shinnah (to use a phonetic spelling) becoming Fox; MacGowan became Smith; MacIntyre (mac an tSaoir) became Carpenter; and McCrosane became Crosbie. Yet there was no clear system of anglicisation or transliteration. O'Connor was changed to Conyers, O'Reilly to Ridley, O'Donnell to Daniel, McCarthy to Carter.

Mistranslations

'In the county of Sligo,' Dr O'Donovan remarks, 'the ancient name of O'Mulclohy has been metamorphosed into Stone, from an idea that *clohy*, the latter part of it, signifies a stone. But this being an incorrect translation in the present instance, these persons may be said to have taken a new name. In the county of Leitrim, the ancient, and by no means obscure, name of Mac Connava has rendered Forde from an erroneous notion that ava, the last part of it, is a corruption of atha, of a ford. In Kerry and Thomond, the ancient name of O'Cnavin is now anglicised Bowen, because *cnáimhin* signifies a small bone. In Tirconnell, the ancient name of O'Mulmoghery is now always rendered Early, because *moch-éirghe* signifies early rising. O'Marchachan is translated Ryder, from *marcach*, signifying a horseman.' It is noteworthy that the Os and the Macs disappeared almost completely from Leinster.

Christian or baptismal names did not fare much better than surnames, usually due to the identification of Irish names with English names to which they were in no way related. Thus we have Aodh (Hugh), Dermot (Jeremy), Mahon (Matthew), Conor (Cornelius), Cormac (Charles), Donnell or Domhnall (Daniel), Brian (Bernard), Flan (Florence), Teigue or Tadhg (Timothy), Donogh (Denis), Turlogh (Terrence), Felim (Felix).

It is useful to reflect on this question: *What precisely is a given person's name?* A society in Dublin recently called upon its members to use 'the Irish version of their names'. Surely a name is a name and cannot have versions? In the Middle Ages learned people and Church dignitaries used their vernacular names for day-to-day colloquy but for formal or solemn occasions used a Latin variant. But in law today it seems a person's name is that appearing on his State birth certificate. Owing to the bother and disorganisation often attending a birth, the name intended occasionally appears on the cert-ificate ludicrously garbled, often entered by a careless doctor or illiterate midwife. This sort of error could have serious consequences. If a generous testator left a fortune to a person cited by his reputed, but officially incorrect, name, he might have trouble getting paid. But this is a comparatively recent hazard. Up to some twenty years ago, persons applying for the old age pension had trouble in establishing that they had in fact reached the age of 70, because the compulsory registration of births was not yet at that time 70 years in force. Baptismal and other parish records did not do much to help. A hair-raising recollection of the Night of the Big Wind was sometimes pressed into service.

Questions, their pleasures and perils

For years I was in the habit of jumping up in great annoyance and switching off the radio when *Question Time* was announced from Dublin. I found the stupidity and obtuseness of most of the competitors very bad for my nerves.

Compere: Number 4, which is the longer, a yard or a league? (Big pause.)

No. Four: A yard. (Gong!)

All the same, all sorts of quiz programmes are still very popular, not only with many radio stations but also as part of stage shows. The Q and A procedure seems to be a deep-seated human neurosis. Practically nothing else goes on in the courts and, of course, we have Question Time in the Dáil itself. Most of us learnt Christian Doctrine through the catechistical method. In regard to that, let me issue a warning. More than once I have heard a heated argument in progress when one of the contestants bellows in a towering rage: 'You see nothing wrong with it? You think it's all right, what? Well if you'd read your penny Catechism, you'd find something different there about it.' I am told that the penny Catechism nowadays costs one shilling and threepence.

Today I am tempted to conduct a small quiz of my own.

Laying Traps

The ideal quiz would contain commonplace questions to which the answer is obvious yet wrong. Here is one:

Q. – Before the buses were introduced in Dublin, did the trams go up Grafton Street?

A. – Not at all.

46

But indeed and they did. They left College Green, went up Grafton Street and turned left into Nassau Street.

Q. – In what county is the city of Waterford?

A. – County Waterford, or course.

No. The Ferrybank part of the city is in Kilkenny. And here is a question which very few people could answer correctly and to which practically everybody would give a No:

Q. – Was there or is there anybody who had a Dublin street or road named after him in his own lifetime?

There was and, happily, is. In Donnybrook there is a thoroughfare of good, red-brick dwellinghouses named Brendan Road. When the brave Batt O'Connor was not busy with operations against the British, he was pursuing his own business as builder and in fact built this whole road. Presumably he named it just as his son Brendan was born, so that it can truthfully be said that Mr Brendan O'Connor, one of the most distinguished architects at present in practice in Dublin, had a public thoroughfare named after him in his native city when he was an infant!

And that is a quare one.

Some Money-Makers

There are a great number of questions on which the interrogator can very safely lay small bets and which depend on the principle that nobody looks at the most familiar objects which are in use and on view every day. How many chicks has the hen on the Irish penny, for instance? But here is one upon which I have made many frugal shillings myself and not once have I got a publican to answer it. If it is asked in a pub, there must be a preliminary warning that the respondent must keep his back to the shelves:

Q. – Two firms named respectively Jameson and Power make whiskey. About the centre of the label in

47

each case, two words appear in very large type. The second word is *Irish*. What is the word before it?

Naturally, there will be a great variety in the answers and the wildest guesses will come from publicans, who have been looking at the bottles in question all their lives. Among the usual words are Irish, Pure, Liqueur, Superfine, Potstill, Best, Guaranteed and Barley. They are all wrong, of course. The word is *Dublin*.

On the usual packet of Player's Navy Cut cigarettes, are there any ships shown? If so, how many? Is there any land visible on the seascape? Is there a lighthouse? Is there a name on the cap of the bearded sailor and, if so, what name? I won't offend the reader by answering questions so easy.

Here is something of a different kind again, but to be done only in a house where there is a telephone.

You casually announce that you have memorised the entire telephone directory. You will be told, no doubt politely, that you are a liar.

With the Phone Book

Very well, you say to some individual, get pencil and paper and write down absolutely any four numbers that come into your head. Don't let me see them. Here, I'll sit over here as far as possible away from you. Have you written the four figures? Good. Now multiply that four-figure number by 9. Have you got a result? Excellent. Now add the figures of the result. Now you have another number as a result of that addition? Right, now get the telephone directory.

You pause here, light a cigarette and tell him to get the page in the directory which bears his last number. If, say, it's page 31, count down the telephone numbers till you reach number 31. You then tell him the telephone number and the name and address of the subscriber.

Explanation: no matter what four numbers he starts

with, if he does what he is instructed to do above, the answer will be 9, 18, 27, or 36. You have, of course, memorised the appropriate entries on those pages. It is easy to see from afar from turn-over of pages which page he is at but it is dangerous to do the job more than twice because the same final number can keep turning up, no matter what the original four were. Try it!

The great danger
of newspapers

What sort of revolution do we like nowadays in this country? Do we like any, or are we tired of that game? Is it a played-out fancy? Worse – is it *uneconomic*?

It may be the heat but various foreign newspapers in front of me have a strange unanimity. Lurid headlines of vast size tell us what we do not wish to hear and what a lot of us do not really understand. CASTRO GRABS ALL, one headline screams. I need hardly stress the fact that there is comment in the use of the word GRABS. It tells readers that Castro is a barbarian and an outlaw. Is he? The matter following is so confused that it gives me no answer. There are mentions of ill-defined 'oil empires'. There is no news as to who owns or controls them, apart from anonymous company titles.

In ill-considered small type the reader is told that for the future petrol is going to be either far dearer or far cheaper. Oil fuel for industry or domestic heating and cooking will be unobtainable.

More Trouble

Another paper, quite unrelated, roars VENEZUELA CHALLENGES THE US. A smaller line reads 'Arrest of Four Marines'. The body of the report contains the disclosure that the men concerned were drunk and disorderly and had assaulted a taxi-driver.

Still another paper trumpets the fact that serious trouble, very likely of a military or aerial character, may be expected as between the US and Canada. The pie presented here is a bit mixed. The US insists on dominating the North American land-mass and objects to protests made by Canadian politicians that they are

'British'. These men have been told by persons of rather indeterminate rank and authority that all that stuff is obsolete and that the continent must be defended integrally. Certain Canadians, no matter how aware of the strategic situation, have replied by singing 'God Save the Queen'.

Keeping pace with this almost comic ill-humour is the grunting and growling as between Khrushchev and what he calls the West. Mentions of the use of nuclear weapons have become as commonplace in this sort of discussion as the bottom of the garden where the praties grow.

The Poles are re-arming, aided by substantial aid from the US. Several other enslaved countries in Eastern Europe are going to rise simultaneously against their Red masters. Germany is getting ready to resume the role (and always with the consent and assistance of the British) of a mighty military power in Europe. Thousands of young Germans are being trained in Britain by the RAF. That soldier's best friend, his rifle, is obsolete. A new machine, far lighter and smaller, is replacing it. It discharges a nuclear missile which can kill in one go a platoon of soldiers or knock out the most modern tank. It can knock down a four-storey house. An organised convergence of them could demolish a medium-sized city and kill everybody in it.

The Black and Tans, who were earnest enough in their endeavours, seem very small stuff compared with this. Indeed, the end of the world, as set forth in the Bible, could justly be said to have been considerably underwritten. Is it all true, or even half true?

Let's Face Facts

Personally, I like to think that most of it is morbid fantasy. It is also modern fantasy and is made possible by comparatively recent advances in the sciences of communication. The primitive newspapers were most

51

unattractive in appearance, hard to read, and usually a few weeks old in reporting events which had occurred in (say) China several months before. Nobody paid any serious attention to newspapers in the centuries I have in mind. Other organs accessible even to illiterates such as sound radio, TV and the cinema, were yet to come, and still a long way off. An approach to humanity in the mass was not possible. Crude admonitions – such as publicly hanging a man for stealing a sheep – were accepted as the best that could be done. Perhaps indeed it was, for democracy had not been heard of and most men had no fundamental rights.

All arguments about the last war apart, I believe Hitler was a lunatic. I believe his astonishing grip on the German and other people was due mainly to the radio. His shrieking was compulsive, and many a time I listened to him myself. His contagion was infective.

But how many of the other lies and fancies I have briefly mentioned above are due to newspapers? I feel the true answer is: Not a few. Reckless newspapers in search of circulation and notoriety can incense bodies of readers to the point of causing a war which would not otherwise, from economic reasons, happen at all.

I think that the record of the Press of this country is clean enough, though it may be mainly because we are a small country and our capacity for originating mischief is small. Still, I think the point I have been trying to make is worth making.

Let's talk of influenza

An old story invented in America concerned a young lady who had to enter hospital for an operation. When she emerged she told all her friends about it and even some strangers. Naturally they were all sympathetic. But she went on talking about this operation all her life, ever embroidering the recital. Eventually she changed even the nature of the ailment for which the operation had been performed. Apparently she could talk of nothing else and in her old age she had the distinction of being the world champion at the art of emptying a room; people slunk away the moment she appeared.

Well, I have had influenza. Why should I not talk about it this once?

The doctor I called when I noticed my soaring temperature first checked that it was nothing really serious such as pneumonia, and said I had influenza.

'I thought,' I said, 'that the main symptoms of that disorder, fever apart, were a sore throat and muscular aches.'

'Ah, no,' he said, 'that thing takes many forms and there is a lot of it knocking around just now.'

That didn't sound very satisfactory. Happily I have a few medical books and decided to investigate this question myself.

What Is Influenza?

I have discovered many surprising things. Doctors and scientists have done much research on it during the last 80 years and have discovered very little that is helpful. The name, based on an Italian phrase, was invented by a man named Huxham in 1743 but there is some evidence that the disease is probably as old as man himself. An illness described by Theocrites in 412 BC has been identified by modern commentators as influenza. It is not generally a dangerous affliction and usually does not last long but there is real danger in complications, by no means rare, such as bronchitis and pneumonia.

Influenza is an acute infectious respiratory disease caused by a filtrable virus. It can enter only via the throat. If this virus in solution were injected into any other part of the body, the heroic volunteer would not get the disease. Scientists DID discover that this virus took two forms, which they dubbed A and B. Apparently both forms are equally bad for you.

What did my own doctor do for me? Nothing at all except tell me to stay in bed. That brings us to another astonishing fact. There is no specific treatment for the virus. Those modern 'wonder-drugs' such as the sulfonamides, pencillin and streptomycin have no effect whatever on this bug.

How does one become infected? Doctors are not sure even about that, though they guess that if one is physically near an infected person, particularly one who is sneezing, the air will be filled with the virus. They also mention the danger of dirty, ill-ventilated rooms or halls (this is probably oblique advice to keep out of the pubs!). Attempts have been made to sterilise the atmosphere in public places but that seems to have been ineffective also. No wonder this malady has been called 'the last of the unconquered scourges'.

The incidence and location of outbreaks is also unpredictable. A severe outbreak is usually fairly localised and is called an epidemic. A pandemic could cover the whole world. Many still alive will remember the pandemic of 1918, which spread over the whole northern hemisphere, killing far more people than lost their lives in the world war then ending. The carnage of war and endemic malnutrition may have had a say in that tragedy – or was it 'flu at all?

But There Is Hope

But the picture is not entirely black. Prophylactic inoculation has been evolved, though again there is no sure knowledge of the duration of the protection the serum affords. I must say I never heard of anybody who sought such injection, though it is only commonsense in a time of epidemic. Can it be that many people do not fear influenza since it is not very painful and really entails a rest in bed for a week?

I almost forgot to mention another real peril of this disease. There is every possibility that a pregnant woman who gets it will have a miscarriage, so that infected people who make no effort to isolate themselves are really public enemies.

Let me conclude with another odd fact. Pigs are also subject to influenza. The books say that the pig virus is not transmissible to humans. I wonder how true that is?

It would surely be a nice how-do-you-do if, after your plate of rashers and sausages in the morning, your temperature shot up to F. 104 and the muscular aches set in.

It would be nice to think that there is really no such thing as influenza and that it is merely a word widely used by doctors when they cannot make out exactly what is wrong with the sick person. But that is a foolish optimism. For the future I'll stick to eggs. Mr Porker can stay away.

Dr Livingstone and the Dark Continent

I hope I offend nobody when I reveal that I have been amused by the imperial adventure of the Irish Army into the Congo, though I admit that the newspapers have overplayed the episode so much that it is beginning to be boring. There have been hundreds of pictures of ferociously-accoutred soldiers kissing goodbye to the wife and babes, reminiscent of Tommy Atkins leaving for the 1914 war. When the 32nd battalion paraded in O'Connell Street, Dublin, tens of thousands lined the route on each side, reminding me of nothing less than the funeral of Michael Collins, though this illusion was a bit spoilt by the pipe band, which also departed for the Congo.

The odd thing is that those green troops, probably not one of whom has ever known combat, have no clear idea of what problem they are expected to solve; neither have their relatives and, for that matter, neither have I. The general notion is that Belgium has relinquished her dominion, cleared out and left the Africans to fend for themselves. As I write, they have not cleared out; thousands of Belgian soldiers are still there, armed to the teeth. Nervous whites in the area have fled to Brazzaville, which is the capital of French Equatorial Africa. Are the French to remain in Africa? Are the UN forces going to impose order on the warring African groups and will the Belgian forces shoot at UN soldiers? Let us agree that the situation is complicated and leave it at that.

Some Facts

The Congo is not a country nor a continent but the second mightiest river on the earth. The Amazon is given first place but this may not be justified. The Congo has a length of over 3,000 miles and far exceeds in majesty the other two mighty African rivers, the Zambesi and the Nile, but Africa is a mass of great rivers, hundreds of which are tributaries of the Congo. Those who take pride in the Shannon as a considerable waterway might note that in parts the Congo is eight miles wide and has many islands. One island is 50 miles long and five miles at its widest part.

The mouth of the Congo was discovered by a Portuguese in 1482 and he erected a pillar there to denote Portuguese dominion, but in the succeeding three centuries scarcely anything was done by way of further exploration or inquiry. In 1816 the British sent a mission under Capt. Tuckey, RN, who found the river and pushed some distance up but some African sickness struck the ship. Tuckey and 16 of his men died and the expedition had to go home.

The Congo basin or drainage area is estimated to be 1,425,000 square miles in area and its possibilities were perceived following Livingstone's discoveries by a man of unique imperial ambitions, King Leopold II of Belgium. His intrusions in Africa began in 1878 and that, so to speak, is where we came in.

The Wonderful Doctor

Dr David Livingstone was a truly incredible person whose feats of travel, endurance and recorded exploration appear to be far outside the capacity of any one man. He was a person of iron constitution and of simple and kindly mind. He was daunted by nothing.

He was born in Lanarkshire in 1813 of poor parents and entered a cotton mill at the age of ten but persisted in a plan of self-education, got eventually to Glasgow and then London where he took a medical degree. His sole ambition was to spread the Gospel in heathen lands and in 1838 he joined the London Missionary Society; he was sent to Africa and went to Bechuanaland where another missionary had set up a station 20 years before. From this centre he started explorations for the seat of another and chose a place 200 miles away, where he built a shack. Here he was attacked by a lion and had his left arm badly injured and so it was to remain for the rest of his life. Here, in a savage land where the natives had never seen a white face and where wild beasts roamed, he sent for his wife.

After two years' missionary work here, he moved with some companions on considerable journeys, his idea being to do pioneering work for missionaries who would follow, recording likely places for new stations and keeping journals which were to be the first real geographic and hydrographic deposit knowledge of Africa. One journey on which he followed the Zambesi to its mouth took two and a half years and enabled the filling in of large tracts of Africa which on the map up till then had been a blank. In 1856 he returned to England very emaciated after his first African stint of 16 years.

On Good Terms

He parted on very good terms with the Missionary Society, for he had now decided that his first duty was to do something about the appalling Arab slave-trading activities he had seen. He took office as Her Majesty's honorary consul in Africa and led an expedition to the Zambesi on HMS *Pearl*, and was joined by his wife and lady missionaries. The geographical fruits of the expedition were enormous, for the intrepid Livingstone penetrated to regions never before seen by a white man. A third expedition, begun in 1865, began with a formidable outfit of sepoys, men, boys, camels, buffaloes, mules and donkeys but the indomitable doctor's urge to keep going forward meant that this retinue had soon dwindled to four boys. He lost his milch goats and his medical chest was stolen so that when fever struck, he was helpless. But he still kept going, staggering or being carried, and at one point received help from Gordon Bennett of the *New York Herald* through H. M. Stanley.

On May 1, 1873, his boys found 'the great master' kneeling at his bed, dead. He was laid to rest in Westminster Abbey.

The question of black

A theme that continues to excite me (and incite me) is the hostility, in certain parts of the world, to coloured people. That phrase 'coloured people' does not make sense apart from denoting that the people are of skin not white. What is the virtue of being white, aside from the well-known judgement that accidents of climate have made for white dominance, and that an ascendancy in technological matters makes it easy for the white man to be boss of the black man?

Would the black man, if populationally ascendent, take steps to make white citizens outcasts? Personally, I don't think so. White people have too many skills to make that sort of segregation possible in a mixed modern community, and those skills seem to be matters, not of personal attainment, but of traditional achievement through trial and error. I have never heard of a negro designing or making a workable motor car but this is not to say that he is incapable of the feat; I feel it means that his interests are elsewhere. Could Henry Ford produce the Book of Kells? Certainly not. He would quarrel initially with the advisability of such a project and then prove it was impossible. Yet it wasn't.

But Those Shoes?

Intrinsically there is nothing wrong with a pair of shoes, properly cared for. They distinguish the gentleman or at least the person who wants to be listed in that class. They carry, however, no guarantees at all. All accomplished crooks are well-dressed and there is a certain risk in being impeccable.

Some people, usually of literary leanings, prefer dirty shoes and suits, unspeakable shirts, and hats that intrude into the area of legend. Perhaps I am wrong but I doubt whether a portrait or paragraph of praise ever appeared in *Vogue* about the late James Joyce. (Now that I think of it, that magazine has never praised myself, perhaps a more serious offence against justice.) This bad temper on my part was induced by a piece which appeared recently in a Dublin paper, sent to it from London. Read it yourself:

> One of the features of London is the army, or so it seems to be, of boot-blacks who ply their trades outside and in such places as Leicester Square. For a shilling, these men will bring the dullest shoes to gleaming perfection. Today in the Hay market, a tall gentleman, complete with pinstripe suit, bowler hat and umbrella, strolled up to a boot-black to have his shoes cleaned. In a moment he was surrounded by a party of at least 100 German tourists, who, never having seen anything like it before, proceeded to take pictures from all angles. The boot-black was pleased, but the elegant gentleman seemed completely oblivious to the goings-on around him.

I hope you do not think it funny. For my own part I feel that it is deeply scandalous; it is also incorrect, tendentious and liable to inflame the passions of people who like to look well in the street or those who just have to. Nobody is going to hand £1,000 to a shabby tramp. Yet who are those people who in London, accoutred with bowler hat and umbrella, dare leave their houses or hotels wearing clean shirts but filthy foot-wear? I think that is a fair question. If they are married men, it seems that their wives refuse to undertake an elementary household chore. If they are visitors in some hotel, it suggests that they have been too lazy or drunk to put their shoes outside the bedroom door on the preceding evening. Any way you look at it, they seem to be thoroughly worthless people.

Cleaning and polishing a pair of male shoes is perhaps the simplest job man can undertake, yet he won't do it, though he thinks nothing at all about unscrewing eight plugs from his car, cleaning them and adjusting the points. He is quite unconcerned about his own spawgs, though they are far more visible and conspicuous than plugs under a bonnet.

In Dublin

I remember the day – it was surely 25 years ago – when about a dozen boot-blacks pursued their trade in College Green in Dublin and under the portico of the Bank of Ireland facing College Street. I was too young and too poor at the time to give them my custom and in any case I think I wore slippers just then. But I could not help noticing them and their uniformly villainous appearance. Men of that type, I concluded, could not possibly be engaged in cleaning other people's shoes. Clearly they were spies – German, British, Irish; some looked bad enough to be serving all those three world powers simultaneously. According to the cutting I have quoted, they have moved to Leicester Square, London, and are now spying for the Russians.

Versatility has always been an Irish virtue.

Let me admit in conclusion that on this whole subject I may be deeply prejudiced. You see, I wear brown shoes and have, in practice, no use at all for boot-blacks. In any case, Sarah cleans my shoes every night. Sarah is my landlady. She knows her duties.

Consequences of having a cigarette

I was standing in the shadow of a great cathedral wall in the days of my youth in company with another cub reporter. Why were we called cubs? My dictionary, in its very rare attempts at cracking jokes, follows up the word CUB with this, in brackets: '(Etymology unknown)'.

But that doesn't matter. More wide-awake than myself, the other cub nudged me and said: 'Better dowse that cigarette. Here's the bishop.'

We were covering a Confirmation ceremony and there is not much to write about concerning that, for the Church is immutable and is ignored by the *Daily Express.*

The bishop completely ignored both of us.

'How well,' I said savagely, 'that thing at my feet looks. It's not a butt but half a cigarette. For all the attention His Lordship paid, we might as well have been smoking cigars. Or long hookah pipes.'

'Aw shut up. Smoking is very bad for you, anyway.'

Are You a Dowser?

Yet out of an ill thing good comes. That phrase 'Dowse that cigarette' stayed in my mind. I thought the verb was incorrectly used and consulted my books of reference, my main idea being, I think, to tell off this unmannerly companion. But I forgot that little grudge when a new world opened before my eyes. True dowsing is nearly supernatural. If you dowse you are beside the gates of heaven, and the word has nothing to do with cigarettes or the equally poisonous activity of working for newspapers.

Dowse is a word I have overlooked, perhaps because

it has an enormous number of local slang equivalents. If one used some of them in mixed company, one might be accused of using bad language and told to leave. If only for that reason, I will forbear giving here a list of the equivalent words. But in usage the word dowse is largely misunderstood, or at least adequately ununderstood. Those who know the word think it is the cunning art of discovering water under the ground by some system of intuition that borders on witchcraft (for which gift decent women used to be roasted alive). My own dictionary, an expensive but notoriously infirm compilation, tells me that a 'dowsing rod' is 'a name for the divining rod' but is starkly silent as to what dowsing is or, indeed, divining. I suppose that so long as there are people in the world, they will publish dictionaries defining what is unknown in terms of something equally unknown. I am personally convinced that Einstein's sums were wrong and that his atom bomb is a myth. Who will blast me out of my complacency? The British needed 100,000 tons of German bombs to blast them out of theirs.

But let us get back to this strange word dowse.

The Great Gift

Dowsing takes its place with soothsaying, curing sick cows by looking at them, and putting a curse on a fellow man. The persons who do that sort of thing – and they are mercifully scarce in towns and cities – do not know where power comes from, why they are thus endowed, but they do know that what they say, be it good or ill, will happen.

Dowsing has that quality. I once spent a term in the Department of Local Government, inhabited at the time mostly by the sons of peasants. The local authority would write asking for permission to pay a gammy, bent, old man to find water. But they were down-faced by what we call (for want of a better word) Education.

'You ought to be aware,' they were sternly told, 'that the modern method of finding is by a geological survey.' A Consulting Engineer had to be got, given twenty-five guineas plus travelling expenses, and his carefully-typed report explained that there was absolutely no water in the county. The local engineer would splutter: 'That dirty tramp up the road in a condemned cottage would find enough water in ten minutes to flood Lough Erin and they wouldn't let me hire him. I'm afraid there is no future for the hazel twig in the Customs House!'

That Twig

One fallacy about dowsing is that the twig or bough must be of hazel. Provided the article is small and flexible, any tree will serve. The important part of it is the man holding it, and about him I can give no description or explanation. The man with this gift of divination is usually very ignorant, occasionally illiterate. Normally he is ignorant of the nature of his trust, and regards it as a bit of a laugh. The ancient Irish attributed great wisdom and insights to the seventh son of a seventh son. Your water-diviner does not bother about genealogy. 'You want to find water?' he says bluntly. 'OK. Give me a few quid and I'll find it within 50 yards of your house.' The terrifying thing is that he does just that.

But my own interest in this theme is broader. The miracle Irishman is narrow-minded and thinks of nothing but water. In fact oil, gold and dead bodies can be discerned.

The word 'dowse' is of Cornish origin, and therefore Celtic. It may seem silly to picture Sherlock Holmes going out for a walk carrying a strange walking stick but if he did so he might solve his mysteries quicker.

A very strange case indeed

Here is a curious news item which the reader may have seen but which I reproduce to jolt the memory:

The largely Scottish settlement of Invercargill, New Zealand, is up in arms. Some unscrupulous character between Britain and Invercargill, the world's southernmost city, has jeopardised the citizens' supply of life blood.

Ten cases, part of a consignment unloaded from the *Sydney Star* at the city's Port Bluff, contained bricks instead of whisky.

Somewhere between the distilleries in Scotland and the last port of call – Liverpool – the whisky bottles had been removed and each case replaced with bricks of an equal weight and neatly packed in straw. New Zealand customs officials are satisfied that the switch did not take place in New Zealand. The bricks are of a type not manufactured in New Zealand.

The switch had the hallmarks of a professional.

I feel several comments are called for here. Did not the agents who received the consignment act rather hastily? How did they know that those bricks were not whiskey? I'm serious. I am sure it is possible to change liquor into a solid form with, of course, a process for re liquifying it if desired (– though, indeed, what's wrong with eating one's booze? A good plate of whiskey and chips might startle our tourists at first but ultimately attract them here in hordes). It is a fact that the fabulous rockets which now traverse space are powered by solid fuel, and it is pretty certain that domestic alcohol can be solidified also. That apart, I am sure that teetotallars will agree that a genuine brick is far more valuable than a bottle of whiskey. If one had enough of them, one could build a house. Who ever heard of a house being built with whiskey bottles? I have heard of houses being brought to ruinous decay with them.

We Should Experiment

In this country we have chemical and physical research bodies, in the universities and elsewhere, and I do think they should be asked to investigate the possibility of converting spirits and even beers into solid concentrates. What is called proof spirit is roughly half pure alcohol and half water. I imagine this water would have to be ignored and the alcohol only changed into cubes of the size, say, of sugar lumps. A person with a whiskey lump could thus, by liquifying it in water just as one melts sugar, have a drink of whatever potency he fancied.

Such factors as bottling, transportation, storage space, warehousing and breakages add materially to the price of whiskey as we know it. The cube system would practically eliminate them all.

And no doubt the new system would bring about many social changes. Reckless fellows would enter a café, order a large black coffee, and quietly drop perhaps half a whiskey cube into it, meditatively stir the cup, and then imbibe. There you would have 'Irish Coffee' with a vengeance! And the cubes could probably be sucked in bed, like sweets.

Also, the whole structure and appearance of pubs would change, becoming perhaps like modest chemist's shops, or beauty parlours. But customers would not be long in getting used to going in and asking for half a pound of whiskey, please. And at festive times it would be seemly to have the cubes on offer in attractive containers, like boxes of chocolates, with a view of the lakes of Killarney or a pretty girl on the lid.

We are too stick-in-the-mud on this subject of liquor. Many drugs can be taken in solid form *per os* or be injected in liquid form. Our present whiskey can be injected, of course, but we should also have the alternative of whiskey tablets, to be swallowed with a draught of water.

A Strange Thief

The passage I have quoted above presents another oddity. Assuming the bricks were not whiskey bricks despatched experimentally by the distillery and were ordinary bricks substituted by the thief for the bottles he stole, why did he bother? It must indeed have been a very troublesome procedure. We are told that the bricks were the same weight as the bottles. This would put the operator to the tedious labour of touring builders' suppliers and construction companies' yards in search of bricks of a specific weight. That alone could be dangerous, even if he was not so foolhardy as to produce a bottle of Scotch and say that he wanted a brick 'of that weight'. My own procedure would be to weigh a bottle carefully and then, quietly at home, make my own concrete block of identical avoirdupois. This method, apart from being safer and trouble-saving, would be far cheaper. Ten cases were filled with bricks instead of whiskey, and that means 120 bricks. I do not know what a good builder's brick costs but if we assume 6d, we are faced with an initial charge of £3. That's plain extravagance.

'The switch,' the report says, 'had the hallmarks of a professional.' Aye, and a very fastidious one. Note that the bricks were neatly packed in straw. Probably he remembered from his schooldays that you cannot have bricks without straw!

Waiting for the imprimatur

Last Friday night I staggered into the machine hall of a Dublin newspaper, clutching a bottle. 'Have a drink, my hearties!' I roared. The men gathered round me holding cups intended for tea and I duly distributed my largesse. Then I began to sing:

> *'Press the button and let*
> *her hum,*
> *Yo Hoe Hoe and a bottle of*
> *rum!'*

For the benefit of the lay reader, I should explain that Hoe is the name of the makers of practically every rotary printing machine in the country.

Nearly every hardship has its concomitant softship. Even influenza, bleak visitation as it is, enables you to loaf luxuriously in bed with a fire in the grate, savour costly hot drinks (with scalding rum at night) and have friends calling to bring you interesting magazines. The younger members of the family stop pestering you for money.

The recent fortnight-long shutdown of the Dublin newspapers was not an unmitigated curse, though it did lead to some queer complaints. One lady said to me resentfully that she had nothing to light the fire with.

In the Home

The stoppage caused certain social changes. One thing it discontinued was the Frigid Breakfast. Here the Husband had the morning paper propped up against the tea cosy, glaring into it in utter silence and completely ignoring the Wife. In the evening occurred Sundown Sulks.

69

The Husband brings home the evening paper which the Wife is very anxious to see. He reads it at his meal, afterwards collapses into a chair by the fire and continues reading it for three hours. This makes the Wife thoroughly cranky. At the end of three hours when it is nearly time for bed, he flings the paper down in disgust.

'Not a damn thing in that paper,' he mutters.

But look at the subject another way. For those accused of breaking the law the non-appearance of the papers was a bonanza. The court on conviction imposes a penalty and takes no account of the often greater penalty involved in having one's name in the papers.

Nobody has any sympathy with a person found guilty of having been drunk in charge of a car, even possibly killing somebody. Passing dud cheques indicates not only a criminal tendency but is proof that the guilty party is a total failure in life, too lazy or incompetent to get a job, and is almost certainly a drunk. One stops asking such a person to the game of cards on Sunday night. Breaking and entering a lock-up shop and stealing cigarettes value £75 and £3–9–412 cash is a truly bad show hardly mitigated by proof that the accused comes from a most respectable family. A bank clerk convicted of stealing £4,662 may get some sympathy (for everybody hates the banks) but it is unlikely that he will get another job.

Yet all that sort of thing was going on every day while the newspaper offices stood dark and mum, and nobody was a whit the wiser. The disorderly classes felt strangely happy and even on the civil side, unseemly litigation between relatives over a will went on, so to speak, in private.

Have We Too Much?

During the stoppage some people complained that their friends were dying and that they knew nothing about it. Well, I don't know that that is so hurtful. Funerals are miserable affairs and mere attendance at one will not bring the bold segocia back to life.

But one cannot help wondering whether we allow the newspaper to take far too big and dominant a place in our lives. Reading newspapers can be an addiction and a neurosis. No other words can explain the pitiful condition of the man who buys several newspapers every day, or those who condoned by purchase the black market which sprang up immediately in London papers, when the *Daily Mail* and *Daily Express* were freely sold out at sixpence per copy.

Let's talk about water

A prosaic subject, you say? Dull? Not at all, but fascinating and strange.

Take a look at the map of the world. It is nearly all water. It is literally true that there is water everywhere, whether in liquid, solid or gaseous disguise. Water is essential for the support of all vegetable and animal life. Apart from being thus essential, it is in human affairs most useful as a solvent and a catalyst. One way or another nearly all water comes from the sea.

Leaving the world aside, take a look at the map of Ireland. It is a small country, surrounded by the sea. Moreover, internally it is waterlogged. It contains an enormous number of rivers, great lakes and those quasi-lakes known as bogs. With water so ubiquitous and plentiful, it might be supposed that the Irish people would have fish as their staple diet, possibly more so than the Eskimos. In fact, however, fish consumption in Ireland is among the lowest in the world.

Penny Herrings

I have never heard any satisfactory explanation of this queer fact beyond one man's emphatic declaration that the Irish simply don't like fish. I do not find that convincing. In the days of my youth in Dublin, the suburban roads resounded with the banshee shrieks of women selling herrings from door to door every Friday morning. For how much? One penny each. And they were fresh herrings, delightful to eat if properly cooked, except for the nuisance of the bones.

How about freshwater fish? To my surprise I find that there are shops here and there where brown trout may be had. I have tried a few from time to time and can certify that they are not fresh: they bear the unmistakable stigmatum of the 'frig.

I like fresh salmon but did not have any this year so far. As I write, the price is 21/- per lb.

Nature of Water

The purest form of water known is snow, and rain the next purest, though rain contains dissolved gases in the atmosphere, carbon dioxide, nitrates, sulphates and ammonia. Those who use rainwater for washing or even drinking find it delightfully soft, almost gentle. And so it is.

What is commonly known as hard water contains salts of calcium and magnesium. Those whose business brings them occasionally to London know all about hard water. A man finds it almost impossible to wash himself or shave, yet Londoners themselves seem to be unaware of their permanent sad plight. And to be fair to them, they do seem duly washed and shaved. A great many of them live, of course, in 'suburbs' which can be as far away as 30 miles from the centre and possibly have a decent local supply.

Water Everywhere

I read recently somewhere that to sustain life, a man must have a daily minimum water intake of two quarts. Most people ridicule this assertion and can prove it is wrong by reciting precisely how much water, or near-water, they do actually consume every day. They have three cups of tea in the morning, three more in the evening and perhaps a bottle of stout at lunch time. How could that build up to two quarts?

The facts will indicate that the matter is not so simple. First, man himself is 80 per cent water; second, if he gets absolutely no water for three days, he will die.

In fact there is water everywhere, even in the hard black coal one puts in the fire.

Take whole milk straight from the cow. The water content of the milk is 87 per cent. You are very fond, of course, of a good sirloin steak after a long cross-country tramp. 60 per cent of it is water. The water content of an egg is 74 per cent. By its very name the watermelon is suspect. Its water content is 92.4 per cent. Naturally, fruit bulges with water. The percentage contained by a peach is 89.4 The cod fish may seem a sound and solid character but 82.6 per cent of him is water.

Weakness for Whiskey

Have you a strong weakness for whiskey? If so, the situation here is quite interesting. You order a glass and put 4/- on the counter. Exactly what is the beaker of yellow stuff that is placed before you?

What is legally defined as proof spirit is roughly 50/50 alcohol and water. It is in that form that spirits are matured in bond. Most whiskeys are now sold at a strength of 30 under proof, which means that 80 per cent of what you are given in your glass is water. With the glass you are given a jug of water. You slosh plenty of this water into the whiskey, bringing the aggregate of water to 90 or even 95 per cent.

True, it is nearly impossible to avoid absorbing water in one form or another. But are you quite sane to be paying four shillings for a modest glasheen of it?

Contemplate the spud!

Discerning readers will be pleased, I hope, that I have not called it 'the humble tuber'.

There is a new word at large, ever oftener to be seen in the newspapers and in the chairman's annual report on the affairs of big and famous companies. It is DIVERSIFICATION. It is not to be confused with, though often allied to, those other disturbing terms TAKE-OVER and MERGER.

In mercantile matters, diversification is a new affirmation of the ancient truth that it is unwise to carry all one's eggs in one basket. The older and more honoured firms, for generations associated with one product and now financially prosperous, have decided that there is no good reason why they should not also engage in manufactures quite other.

A Good Example

The firm of Guinness is a good example. For nearly two centuries they were world famous for making brown stout. Their first small departure was in marketing Gye, a yeast extract. In recent years they have begun brewing ale and lager in a big way. They have fused with the British brewers Ind Coope, apparently mostly for the reason that Guinness will have access to the thousands of 'tied houses' that concern operates in Britain. All that is within the drink business. But Guinness have also entered into a sort of partnership with a big drug firm. They also make furniture and (believe it or not, for this sounds like whimsy, with the bells of Santa Claus's reindeer sounding faintly in the distance) they own the firm of Callard and Bowser, the famous Scottish makers – or inventors? – of butterscotch. In a less industrial mood, the firm also subsidises the writing of poetry. This type of development is enormously widespread. The Glaxo firm, who began with making a baby food in a small way, is now a giant among the manufacturers of drugs and pharmaceutical products. I am not sure that the people who produce Beechams Pills do not also make motor cars.

The Sugar Daddy

The Irish Sugar Company, a quasi-State concern, has taken it into its head that there is more to life than merely making sugar. For some time now they have been engaged in promoting the growing of fruit by farmers for canning, with a special eye on the export market.

The latest announcement has been that the company is installing at Tuam a plant for the manufacture of potato flakes and that it expects to be in a position to process 5,000 tons of potatoes this year. Potato flakes? I had never heard the term and at first took it to be a gentlemanly name for crisps, so widely sold in paper bags over the counters of pubs and other refuges. But no. It is a way with potatoes recently patented in the US and the official announcement says that the process 'results in a product giving high-grade mashed potato by the addition only of hot water, milk and butter'. Not for the first time, I confess that I am a bit mystified by the notions of my betters. Is there something wrong with the century-old fashion of boiling potatoes, mashing them, impregnating the mash with parsley and serving piping hot with butter? Must the most familiar and durable food on earth also be 'processed' and, in Ireland particularly, should it be served with stewed steak marketed in cans?

I cannot repress a strong suspicion that in the whole spectrum of human food, the laboratory technicians are going off their heads, aiming at the day when all eatables will be treated and interfered with in some way and that the ultimate aim is to make the cultivation of the little garden at home illegal. Even the water in the tap in Dublin is not safe; violent controversy rages over a proposal by the Department of Health to compel the Corporation to charge the water with fluorine, a chemical denounced by many world authorities as cumulative in effect and often proved lethal.

Our Staple Food

In Ireland for some centuries now the potato has been the fundamental, nonperishable food for man and beast and has become, indeed, an ingredient of Irish history. Nobody can say when the potato reached Ireland or even Europe; the old Irish records make no mention of it, grains being the basic root crop. The potato as we know it (not the sweet potato) seems to have been indigenous in South America and from there reached North America. Sir Walter Raleigh is credited with having brought the potato to Britain – and thus to Ireland – from Virginia in 1585, but it was unknown in Virginia until a century later.

Not total shortage of food, for food was being exported at the time, but the failure of the potato crop caused the famine in 1846/7, which in effect means that millions of the Irish people were in fact living on potatoes, and proving to be physically fine and long-lived specimens. In the vitamin-infested paradise of chemistry, this fact tends to be ignored. The disease was a fungoid visitation known as late blight. If one takes a global and serial concept of human destiny, the famine here, despite its horrors, was not an unmixed disaster. It accelerated the growth of the New World and the spread of this country's name and influence everywhere.

The farmer or the modest gardener who grows this most handy food is often quite unaware of the astonishing number of enemies the potato plant has.

There are virus diseases (mild, latent and rugose mosaic, leaf roll, spindle tuber and yellow dwarf); fungus diseases (early blight, late blight, scab, fusaria, black scurf, wart); bacterial diseases (blackleg, brown and ring rot) and heavens! – insects. Ever hear of the Colorado Beetle? But I am straying into the parish of Colleague Lea.

The written word

In this season of thought and recollection I think I will write about writing. It may seem a silly subject but it is far from that. In fact writing is very important. As they say in Latin, the written word remains. Generally this is not true of the spoken word. But if the spoken word is repeated often enough, it is eventually written and thus made permanent – or in the photographer's sense, 'fixed' for good. Many a decent man who has written a bad cheque knows the truth of that.

A great many people who perhaps have not given the subject much thought are quite mistaken on this subject of literacy, or the ability to read and write. Nowadays nearly everybody can do that, yet this universal competence is scarcely a century old. And indeed I must withdraw that word 'universal'. The last competent estimate made said that 60 per cent of the world's population (or 820,000,000 persons) were illiterate. A side-detail is that in any illiterate community, far more females than males have that bookless failing. There are still enormous tracts of this earth to which what we call democracy has not penetrated, and where 'equality of the sexes' would be regarded as a painful joke.

Yet that situation is not uniformly glum. Writing, typing, mechanical dictation or even printing does not necessarily confer wisdom on that character who calls himself *homo sapiens*. Sometimes one or other of those arts merely proves that he is an ass. I am sure our venerable Censorship Board will bear me out there. Their point is that it is a pity he never learnt the other art of shutting up.

Does the Press Impress?

This subject is recondite, even mysterious. Before people who can claim to be reasonably civilised learnt to read and write, and certainly long before they had been suborned into taking notice of that chatterbox, the radio set, they had other resources now long fallen into disuse. They had impeccable memories. They could buy or sell a beast at a fair with absolutely nothing in writing. It may be that they could not read or understand a word on the bank notes which changed hands, but anybody who tried to speak decorously and decently, knew their prayers, and had always an acute political sense. Even if they are so backward as to be able to make nothing of the figures on the calendar on the wall, too well they know the day of the week it is, the year and even the century. The *Encyclopaedia Britannica* is not too far ahead of them at all.

A handy example of this phenomenon is still to be found in Ireland, though the sinister National Schools tend to erode it. I mean the Gaeltacht areas which still tenuously survive here. Far from being an insult, it is a compliment to say that the really older people are illiterate; yet they can speak accurately, frequently with a strange felicity, which is probably the most highly inflected language still spoken in Europe (or anywhere else for that matter) and can recite tales which take a week of nights in the telling. They do not appear to the stranger to be under any disability. Even when they catch some sickness – which they rarely do – usually they do not have to send for a doctor. They know the cure, too, horrified though the doctor might be if he heard what it was. These utterly self-sufficient mammals are gradually disappearing, even from the ruder and braver parts of our country. Thanks be to goodness, we have still a good way to go before we are in the same shape as the good people of Britain, where it was discovered, on the introduction of socialised medicine, that nearly everybody was sick.

The Print Drug

It would be an interesting task for some indefatigable researcher (not me, not today) to try to investigate the effect of the printed word on any given country's political and social norm. In Germany Hitler's initial impact on the people was not with revolvers, machine-guns or nooses but with fountain pen and typewriter. He knew that the mind was a more important target than the body at the beginning, though, as one who at the start, and equipped with doubtful German, gingerly made my way through *Mein Kampf*, I kept wondering whether he was trying to bulldoze the nation or reform it. He was by no means the first demagogue, however, to be incoherent.

This subject of writing has recently been otherwise in the news. A group of Protestant divines in Britain have issued a 'modern' re-write of the New Testament. I confess I have not read it but have seen several extracts from the text in responsible London papers denouncing it. One witty commentator recalled that Hamlet had not been written by any committee. This remark is more apt than may at first appear, for if the English of the Bible as heretofore accepted is archaic, how about Shakespeare himself? Should Robert Graves, the new Professor of English at Oxford, re-write Hamlet or, as the Americans might say, louse it up? Or why not put Homer's work into the broken-up jargon that is modern Greek?

The foregoing is a rather elaborate way of revealing that I have just written a book myself. That may give the reader some notion of how disoccupied I am. I did this job, on top of sundry other chores, in exactly eight weeks, and I claim that that alone is evidence of considerable industry.

Will it be published? Yes indeed, possibly this year. What is it about? That question is foolish. We modern writers have moved away from the ancient idea that a book must be *about* something. What do you expect to get for your fifteen bob anyway? A scheme for growing tomatoes in window boxes? How to make your own TV set? Heavens – a plot?

Those decent folk
– my friends

Are your friends as good as MY friends? I can discern the nod of assent but doubt it. My own friends are far better, they are famous people and they are all dead.

Who, you may ask, are those friends of mine, and why are they dead?

It is a fair question. They are dead because, had they lived, they would have been very old and would have died anyway from extreme old age and decrepitude.

One of my friends is Shakespeare.

Is that enough? Do I have to add that another is Homer? Horace I claim as an acquaintance. Father Peter O'Leary was a cousin on the mother's side, and Rabelais was supposed to have been a great-great-great-great uncle.

Some Other Friends

My science of friendship is capable of unlimited expansion. Any second-hand bookshop is all I need to make still another new friend. Even my wife occasionally brings home a new pal in her handbag, though her associates are not necessarily mine. Indeed, I find it hard to get on with some of them, being uneasy in their presence and not understanding wholly the English that they talk. I cannot make head or tail of Edgar Wallace, for example, and Ethel M. Dell is to me an utter mystery. Trollope? Yes, he lives nearby and we exchange coldish nods. Believe it or not, one of my choicest butties is Alexander Pope. The only man I cannot stick at all is Oliver Goldsmith. I cannot quite understand my dislike here. Goldsmith was a decent man and did his best to write good English but I have absolutely failed to get fond of him. Plain hatred is what

I entertain for Sir Samuel Ferguson. His *Lays of the Gael and Gall* is a disgusting anthology, a monument of home-made decay. A terrible rage boils up within me if anybody within my hearing mentions Wordsworth. I cannot comprehend why that man was ever called into existence. I take the easy course of assuming he is an absurdity and possibly never lived at all, being invented by some person with an imagination on the macabre side. It is inconceivable that he had a mother, for all women are intrinsically virtuous.

And will your heart fail, good reader, if I mention Sir Walter Scott? I read his autobiography once upon a time and am not yet the better of that experience. He explained to me in quite unnecessary detail that he had once accidentally managed to owe another person £100,000, and then proceeded to pay this sum off. He succeeded but did not eat much food for many years. In this interval he wrote the terrifying Waverley Novels, causing several persons who never hurt him to incur the disease known as dementia.

Recently I passed by a book-shop in Nassau Street Dublin, except I didn't pass by. Unhappily, I paused. The damned sixpenny barrow lured me. I am fatally fond of big thick, fat books. They seem great value, irrespective of content.

Weighty Volume

At this sixpenny barrow I bought the autobiography, in two volumes, of Henry Taylor. When I got the books home, I weighed them on my wife's balance in the kitchen and they weigh four and a quarter pounds. I have never heard of Henry Taylor but the books were published in 1885 by Longmans, Green and Co. I have not read Mr Taylor's account of himself but a furtive glance at one volume gives me the suspicion that this man was a poet, or thought he was. A frontispiece portrait shows him looking very old and sporting an enormous white wig. Why did he waste so much valuable time growing so very old and writing that poetry that nobody nowadays reads and probably never read?

The subtitle of the first volume intrigues me. Just this modest phrase – 'Vol. I: 1800–1844'. Forty-four years of abject futility, squeezed into one volume, weighing over two pounds avoirdupois.

Thoughts on the yoke

A question the reader may ask is 'What do you mean by "the yoke"?' Let us go to the dictionary for the answer.

'YOKE – from a root (Latin *jungo*, I join) meaning to join. A part of the gear or tackle of draught animals, particularly oxen, passing across their necks; a pair of draught animals yoked together; something resembling a yoke in form or use; a frame to fit the neck and shoulders of a person for carrying pails or the like; fig. servitude, slavery.'

The early motor car was known as 'the horseless carriage' and that is why the car came to be known, at least in Ireland, as the yoke. My thoughts on the yoke this week arose from a conversation I had with an intelligent and educated man, himself a yoke-owner, who flabbergasted me by saying that the motor car had been invented by Henry Ford. It is an astonishing fact that most car-owners are nearly totally ignorant about their cars – a fact, alas, which some ruffianly garage owners turn to good account. I have heard of one such man who sold a charming lady who drove up in a Volkswagen (which is air-cooled) a tin of anti-freeze fluid. One other new VW owner, asked by a friend how the car was going, said it was going very well. 'Don't mention this to a soul,' he added, 'but I have made a discovery. *There is no engine in it!*'

How It Began

The first 'horseless carriage' was not the motor car as we know it. A Frenchman named Cugot built about 1771 road carriages operated by steam. In the years which followed, many others throughout the world made their own steam cars. But from 1831 the English parliament decided that those vehicles were unpleasant and dangerous and enacted the notorious Red Flag laws which compelled anybody driving a steam road carriage to be preceded by a man carrying a red flag by day or a red lantern by night. Other crippling disabilities such as penal tolls exacted by highway authorities practically killed the steam car in Britain, and the law establishing the spectre with the red flag was not repealed until 1896.

But in Germany and France the possibilities of the internal combustion engine were under study. About 1885 Gottlieb Daimler in Germany patented his high-speed internal combustion engine, and is commonly credited with being the inventor of the motor car, fundamentally as we know it. But there is some dispute here. Karl Benz and Siegfried Marcus are credited with having built comparable vehicles about the same time. The truth is that the motor car was not invented by any individual but was the result of the talent of many men over a long space of time.

Ford's first car appeared in 1893; by 1940 the company had produced more than 28,000,000 cars. His great achievement was to invent mass production on the assembly-line system, and he deserves a special article to himself; he was a crank who made crankshafts.

Its Effect on People

The motor car, in its extreme youth, was commonly regarded with naked hostility; it frightened horses and even frightened people because in its early days its gear system was such that when it encountered a steep hill, it had to ascend it backwards. At best, enlightened people regarded it as an ingenious toy. It is curious that the primitive cars were regarded by many as a means of sport and racing, not until much later to be accepted as a means of fast, everyday transport for man and goods.

Its coming entailed, at least in what are called

civilised communities, a real and spectacular revolution, the more so when one remembers that the aeroplane was the son of the motor car. And it was not merely a mechanical revolution. The car had a formidable social impact. One of the early objections to it was that it raised blinding clouds of dust in dry weather. The thoroughfares of long ago were not roads at all in the present sense. The car created the modern road. It enabled people to live away from slums and city congestion and brought into being whole new communities.

A social change? Some people think that the motor car is, possibly next to gunpowder, the greatest curse which has ever descended on mankind. They hold that a yoke is as directly related to strong liquor as is a glass and that all car drivers are nearly always stotious. That is great exaggeration but it is true that death and injury attributable to the yoke, while reducible with care on everybody's part, is inevitable. Danger is implicit in any sort of movement. In London resides a valuable body known as the Royal Society for the Prevention of Accidents. Where has it been statistically established that most accidents, fatal and otherwise, happen?

In the home. The sad fact is that we are mortal and are safe nowhere. Even if the extreme step of bringing back the man with the red flag were taken, I'm sure there would be a fatal accident. The yoke following him would run him down and kill him.

The Model T man

Some weeks ago I promised to write something about Henry Ford (1863–1947), if only because I have been reading about him recently. Isn't it hard to believe that he was alive as late as 1947?

He was an extraordinary man. He knew more, at least in his earlier days, about litigation than he did about automobiles. He had also a formidable grasp of the law governing patent rights in his time, and made this known several times by firing lawyers who told him he was wrong.

A recital here of his monstrous litigations would be not only dull but probably incomprehensible. To put it briefly, Ford was an eccentric man who had nonetheless many sound ideas, not a few of them since adopted universally. He was, to use a cliché, ahead of his time and he naturally suffered from it. A life-span of 84 need dismay no man. He seemed as indestructible as his famous Model T.

His Beginnings

The deep thinking on large-scale industrial problems which were to characterise Ford's life had indeed simple beginnings. Though born on a farm near Dearborn, Michigan, his parents had emigrated from Cork in 1847. That was one of the famine years, and the trip must have been a painful and squalid passage in a wind-jammer, with no hint that it would conclude in the mass manufacture of the 'flivver'. Yet that is what did happen. Tradition has it that the Ford factory in Cork, originally intended for the manufacture of agricultural tractors, was founded by Ford in memory of his parents. Very likely that is true. The iron structure of

Ford's mind did not exclude sentiment.

Yet his parents do not seem to have been true Irish people at all, not that it matters when one considers his life-work. His mother's name was Mary Litogot and, born in the US, had Dutch parents herself. William Ford, the father, was probably of English extraction. The mother died when Henry was 12, and William decided that his son should be a farmer. His main interest as a youngster was in mechanics, taking asunder at the age of 13 a watch and then correctly re-assembling it. His main tool was a knitting needle, flattened at the point to a very keen blade. Although compelled to do farm work by day and no excuse taken, Ford spent many hours at night mending watches and thus sustaining his interest in machines, besides quietly making some money.

Just when and how did he go into the motor business? This is not certain, but his first vehicle was a farm tractor worked by a steam engine which was, in fact, far too heavy for the job. His father, to put a stop to this nonsense, offered Henry a 40 acre farm, much of it wooded. Henry built a saw mill worked by steam, cut the trees and sold lumber. About 1888, taking advantage of his comparative independence, he got a job with the Detroit Edison Company as an engineer and it was about this time that he began to experiment with the petrol engine, somewhat as we know it today. He formed the Ford Motor Company in 1903 with a capital of 100,000 dollars and the first cars he made and sold, designed solely for speed, won every race for which they were entered. That is one of the ironies of the story. The origin of motoring rests, not on universal trans-portation but on racing.

What Conclusion?

What is one to make of the whole story? It is not easy to say, at least by those who have a poor grasp of staggering figures. Ford ignored trade unions but paid a far higher rate than the minimum they prescribed. He refused to enter into any agreements or conventions with other motor-makers. As his organisation developed, he did not see why he should pay merchants or middlemen for timber; so he bought, maintained and developed his own forests. He equally disdained shipping companies and soon had his own vessels for transportation of his cars overseas. Later he was to realise that this transportation was in itself wasteful and that his cars should be made or assembled at various spots throughout the world. In the United States alone he founded 34 assembly plants and now Ford factories exist in many parts of the world, manned almost wholly by natives.

Talking of Dr Diesel

Having written last week about Henry Ford and his famous Model T, I feel I should say something this week about the diesel engine. The theme is gruesomely topical, for the Eichmann trial has revealed that one of the 'quick and easy' methods of murdering Jews, locked in a road truck, was to divert the exhaust gas of its diesel engine into it. The irony of that sort of tragic killing lies in the fact that the inventor of the diesel engine was a German.

Some of the books say he wasn't, for he was born in Paris in 1858. But both his parents were German, and nearly all his education took place in Munich. A technical paper he published, in English named *The Theory and Construction of a Rational Heat Motor*, led to the making of the first engine by Rudolf Diesel, and to the diffusion of the principle he discovered today throughout the world. The engine was first publicly shown in Munich in 1898, and in the same year an American (?) named Busch paid Diesel one million gold marks for the rights of US manufacture. The soundness of his idea was self-evident.

Rudolf Diesel's life (1858–1913) was ended in a way not to be expected in the regime of a skilled and original engineer. On the night of September 29–30, he fell off the Antwerp-Harwich steamer and was drowned.

The Diesel Principle

Most of us have a fair idea of how the petrol engine works. A mixture in the form of gas prepared in the carburettor in the air-fuel ratio of 14.5:1 is introduced to the cylinders and exploded by means of sparking plugs, which are activated by an intricate electrical system.

Diesel knew from miscellaneous experience that compression itself meant the spectacular generation of heat and the principle of his engine is based on the theory that the sparking plug is not necessary to achieve combustion. In his cylinder, ordinary air is compressed to about 500 lb per square inch, which raises its temperature to 1000 F. This has been defined as red-hot air, and into it is injected a spray of atomised oil. There is an instant explosion. The event is spontaneous, and the machine begins to work.

Yet the diesel engine has certain inherent delicacies. In this country the steam engine, having served faithfully for a century, is steadily being ousted by diesel locomotives, and never have traction breakdowns been so frequent. The steam engine has always been a notoriously inefficient machine, a great amount of its energy being spent on moving itself; it has been a sort of diabolical creature, breathing fire, shaking the earth and causing enormous uproar. But its sheer brute-strength made it the pivot of a whole era, just as Henry Ford's Model T was later to do.

Is Petrol Obsolete?

Nowadays several makes of car are offered with, at the option of the purchaser, petrol or diesel engines. Some people think petrol is on the way out, for the cost of unearthing, transporting and refining it is vastly higher than the crude stuff a diesel engine uses. This is indeed a half-truth. The petrol engine is far more versatile than the diesel, universally understood and capable of being serviced anywhere. On the other hand, the diesel is more suitable and economic for really heavy work such as driving ships, moving earth, powering military tanks, or driving the machinery of great factories.

Man has not yet found the ideal method suitable for

all purposes, though he seems to have decided that steam will no longer do.

There are still in the far corners of Ireland the quiet man who thinks he found the true answer when he was a little boy, and still believes in that answer. It does not entail crankshaft, injectors or plugs. You just get a simple cart and yoke a donkey into it.

The folly of the answer game

I am sure many readers share my horror of the quiz. It is a useless and infuriating abomination, and it is infernally ubiquitous. One can scarcely take up any magazine or newspaper (*The Nationalist and Leinster Times* honourably excepted) without encountering it in one form or another. Versions of it occur on the cinema screen. Turning on the radio is a matter of deadly risk. When I personally do so, I am almost certain to hear the voice of my friend, Joe Linnane.

'Now, Number One. This is a six-mark question. How much are two and two? If you add two and two together, what do you get?'

(Pause).

'Em . . . five.'

'No. Hard luck, Number One. The correct answer is four.'

(This last, as an absolute statement, is in fact wrong. There are fluids, also gases, which when combined equally in two-part quantities, do not achieve a total of 4 but sometimes as low as 3½ because the combination brings about a change in the overall molecular structure.)

Crosswords, the yo-yo and whistling in the bus are all bad. But the quiz is worst of all.

Is It Good For You?

The firm of Guinness is world-renowned, chiefly for the gift of making good stout and producing sundry kindred brews. Quite recently they have seemed to have gone wild and produced a massive book of 280 large pages. A treatise on brewing? Not at all, but the answers to quiz questions on every subject under the sun, a unique compendium of useless knowlege. There is scarcely any mention of Guinness itself except an oblique one when, having disclosed that the largest brewery in the world is in the US, it adds that the largest in Europe is none other than Arthur Guinness, Son and Company Ltd.

Which is the largest airline in the world – TWA or Pan-American? Neither. It is the Russian airline 'Aeroflot', which operates 1,006 aircraft.

Which distinguished singer earned most in the course of his career? Caruso, of course. No, no, you are wrong. It was our own John MacCormack, who piled up a total of £1,400,000.

Still talking of music, this book can be funny, though the editors swear every word they print is true. It is useless asking the reader where and when was the vastest orchestra ever assembled, what sort were the instruments and how many of them were there. The respective answers are Trondheim, Norway, August, 1958; brass 12,600. Is this true? I cannot help doubting it, for I was in this country in 1958 and in my health and I did not hear the recital.

A Few More Facts

It is impossible to give the reader a true notion of this remarkable compendium but I will quote a few more facts entirely at random. The palm for prodigious literary output goes to an American, Eric Stanley Gardner, aged 70. He dictates up to 10,000 words a day and is usually engaged on seven novels simultaneously. What I personally admire here is not so much the output as the uncanny control which prevents a character in one book from accidentally straying into another and thus snarling up both books.

The highest spire in the world is that of the Protestant cathedral at Ulm, Germany; 528 feet. St Paul's in London was a mere 489 feet but was struck by lightning in 1561. (I did not know St Paul's existed then.)

But when it comes to a question of ecclesiastical age, we need not bang our own heads. The Gallerus Oratorio near Kilmalkedar, Co. Kerry, reputedly dates from AD 550!

The heaviest beer-drinking country in the world is Belgium.

Between 1940 and 1955 a number of 'counter-revolutionaries' were executed in China. How many? At least 20 million.

The last public hanging in London was in 1868, the distinguished main actor being Michael Barrett, a Fenian.

The country with most psychiatrists (13,425) – it's an easy guess – the United States.

One more Guinness

Does stating something as a fact make it true? That is a more complicated question than it sounds, for what begins as lie can in time become truth. When Hitler told the German people, for purposes of his own, that Germany's dearest friend was the Soviet Union, he was believed and Germans in general became very friendly with Russians. That both nations tried later on to exterminate each other is irrelevant. The mutual esteem, while it lasted, was genuine.

This week I return, as threatened, to the *Guinness Book of Records*. This book is full of extraordinary allegations, for the veracity of which no source or proof is given. On the other hand, there is no reason to suppose that this majestic firm should go out of its way to circulate a parcel of lies. We must take the material on trust, as we do the contents of newspapers.

The Mostest

In the matter of printed books, the bestseller of this era was *Gone With the Wind* by Margaret Mitchell. It deals with the American Civil War and has become so well-known that it is casually referred to in many publications merely as GWTW. Twenty years ago I felt I must be stupid and illiterate for not having bought and read it. I bought a copy all right but in the course of four heroic attempts to read it I broke down. Frankly, I found it unreadable, badly written, dull.

Hollywood nearly strangled itself in an effort to make it the greatest film ever. Even the film I found dull, ridiculously elaborate and far too long. I do not doubt that the fault is in myself.

Turning to the *Guinness Book*, there is a statistic

concerning the longest run of a play. The play in question opened in Los Angeles on July 6, 1933, and, playing one show a night, lasted until September 6, 1953. The title of this play? *The Drunkard.*

The reader may well ask why it stopped at all after over twenty years. The answer is that it didn't. The play was made the subject of a musical adaptation called *Wayward Way* and this piece was played on alternate nights with the original until October 1959. When finally discontinued, *The Drunkard* had been played 9,477 times.

I feel there must be a moral buried here. For some people drink itself is a fascination but for a far greater number, all total abstainers, the subject of drink and drunkenness fascinates. No doubt *The Drunkard* is a burlesque and funny in its own right, like *Ten Nights in a Bar-room* as played in Dublin years ago by the Edwards-MacLiammoir company. All the same, I cannot think of any other theme that could stand up to the harrowing friction of a 26 years' run. No doubt the players themselves had to be changed, for one who was a pretty young lady at the start would have become a middle-aged matron by the end.

Other Strange Facts

The heaviest bell in the world is known as the Tsar Kolokol, cast in Moscow in 1733. It weighs 193 tons and is not to be mentioned in the same breath as the heaviest in Britain, the Great Paul in St Paul's, London, a toy that weighs a mere 16 tons.

In the US, an outfit named Kraft Foods entered into a contract with the singer Perry Como (48) for a one-hour appearance daily on colour television. Including production expenses, the money involved was £8,928,000. This seems to prove we are all in the wrong country.

The largest store in the world is R.H. Macy of

Broadway. I will not trouble the reader with details of the staggering daily sales beyond saying that it has 11,000 employees. The floor space is 46.2 acres, and I do not find it feasible to work out how many times bigger this is than Croke Park.

Talking again of shops, what is the longest chain of chain-shops? In the US there is an enterprise known by the long-winded name of The Great Atlantic and Pacific Tea Company; they have 120,000 employees, 4,276 branches, and operate two laundries of their own for dealing with the workers' uniforms. Outside the four county boroughs, no town in Ireland has anything like the population of the GA & PT's staff. Maybe it is just as well.

The largest tractor in the world (naturally a product of the US) was exhibited in May last year. It weighs 50 tons.

This *Guinness Book* is getting under my nails. Very likely I will be back to it again next week.

As noble as our newspapers

A newspaper is like the man: it behaves itself, does not print scandalous matter, achieves dignity, worships truth, and refrains from libel. Most of us would like to be men as noble as our newspapers.

A friend recently gave me a copy of the *Evening News*. Dublin people are mightily surprised that London, a town with a population approaching 9,000,000, has only two evening papers, whereas Dublin has three. It makes no difference. The contents are the same. Even the type-faces don't vary.

First Issue

This copy of the *Evening News*, still going strong, was presented to readers on Tuesday, July 26, bearing the date 1881. It was a reproduction of the first issue of a publication that prospered. It is a curious thing to look at in 1961. Very different people from us must have read it. And they must have had better eyes.

It is not too easy to isolate what is different about it, apart from some obvious physical things. I should say that the main differences lay in editorial attitude. The news was presented with a take-it-or-leave-it gesture. It didn't matter very much. Neither did the reader.

No Headlines

Perhaps the most impressive fact about the publication was the absence of display type. There were no headlines. The death of a dog in Hammersmith got the same show as the suicide of the head of a ruling house in Europe. Ireland was never mentioned at all, but plenty of space was given to cricket.

Absence of display type meant that births, marriages and deaths got mixed up with mattresses, honey, and goings-on in South Africa. In that year of 1881, it will be recalled, the Queen was on the throne. Mr Gladstone was performing in the House of Commons. It was the Age of Peace, at least for Britain. The great Empire was still there.

Yet that paper shows some curiosities. I don't mean that it announces its price as one halfpenny (as it does) but hints at a different social attitude. Everything is mentioned in monotone, as if it did not matter very much. Generally, one feels that the *Evening News* of 1881 is very different from today's *Daily Express*. Is it better? It is not easy to answer that question. I would say it is more restful. It would be unlikely to give you a heart attack in bed in the morning.

Siberian Plague

No occurrence, however catastrophic, rated a greater display than the upper case of the text, or just plain capital letters. Thus one read a heading such as Outbreak of Siberian Plague without being unduly disturbed. Another report was headed Punishment at Sea. Still another – please remember the date – was headed The Russian Imperial Family.

News reports are announced as 'Telegrams', thus paying tribute to the new invention, and there is an enormous, very heavy leading article about the Transvaal. There were no features, no glimpse of the common man.

Yet perhaps he did intrude a little bit.

One man inserted a notice saying that he was selling first quality salt. That was fair enough, and several other people were doing the same. But this man said that there was a reduction in price of 10 per cent for total abstainers.

I think I had better end here.

The world is right-handed

I think I mentioned some weeks ago that I had smashed my right fore-arm. It may be that a person who expatiates on such an injury is to be likened to the lady who talks endlessly and minutely (for at least forty years, anyhow) about her operation, conferring excruciating boredom on her listeners and making them want to run away.

I don't think, however, that the two situations are identical. For instance, no operation lasts for several weeks and in practice, anybody who undergoes a serious operation can know nothing about it.

Twin Organs

I may be permitted initially a few general observations. The human being is fitted out with certain twin organs such, for example, as the arms, legs, eyes, ears, kidneys, lungs. It is unprecedented for each of the twins to operate with equal efficiency.

Everybody has a master eye. How often does a companion say to us: 'Walk on this side of me. I'm deaf in the left ear.' Disease frequently appears in one lung and not in the other, and this is also true of the kidneys.

Ambidexterity, or the use of either hand with equal ease, is more a word than a fact. Even skilled and well-trained boxers do not have it. Biologists have often recommended that children should be meticulously trained in ambidexterity but since it is the left hemisphere of the brain which controls the motor apparatus of the right side of the body, other commentators have said that the equal development of the right hemisphere would cause speech impediment.

Got a Hiding

In practice, what happened when we were all very young? Those of us who showed a clear tendency to use the left hand as the primary corporal tool got a severe hiding for our pains. All the same, there are many left-handed people in the world – particularly, for some reason, cricketers. The 'normal' person's left hand and arm is almost quite useless except for assisting the right.

If, however, one closely observes a person who is well and truly left-handed, one soon notices that his right hand is by no means as useless as the 'normal' person's left. It has a real though diminished usefulness. I think I know why.

Are parents who sternly discourage a left-handed attitude on the part of their children ignorant and eccentric people? I do not think so. They are really trying to save the child from a lifetime of inconvenience, and even situations of physical danger. The reason is that the whole world is organised on the basis that everybody is right-handed. That is why left-handed adults must put the right hand to some use, whether they like it or not, and attain gradually a certain proficiency in its use.

To put the fore-arm in plaster from the elbow, it is necessary to continue the iron dressing down to the knuckles in order to obtain anchorage at the seat of the thumb. That usually immobilises the whole hand and the fingers. I soon found what this meant.

Like most gents, to wash myself I used nothing more than water, soap and my two hands. Well, I could not wash myself. Preposterous licks with a left-handed cloth may have removed some of the more striking filth. But that was merely to confront me with another ordeal – shaving.

Plain Impossible

This was a very lengthy and terrifying business, with great blood losses, and a finished job that looked just awful. Then putting on a shirt, manipulating studs to fix a collar, and finally knotting a tie – that was plain impossible.

Discarding all pride, I had to call in my consort, to discover, however, that she did not know how to knot a tie, though some lessons soon fixed that. And lacing shoes was another task beyond me.

Later, I found that a bus is designed for the right hand as to mounting it, dismounting and finding a seat. There was infinite danger in a bus trip. A meal which entailed use of a knife and fork was impossible. Even lighting and smoking a cigarette was perilous. I had to give up completely playing billiards, the violin and the piano. And typing with the left hand only is infinitely arduous.

Are you curious about all this, dear reader, or even incredulous? Why not find out? For a trifling cost, any chemist will put your own right arm, from elbow to knuckles, in pitiless plaster. Then heaven help you, and me too, if we manage to get mixed up in a rough house.

What's funny?

That question is serious. Just what makes us laugh? I once asked a celebrated physician what a sneeze was. He began giving me a lengthy piece of rawmaish about the windpipe, the throat, the larynx and the lungs. I cut him short.

'Doctor,' I said, 'you are describing the location of the sneeze. I asked you about the event itself.'

After a pause, he said:

'A sneeze is a paroxysm, and quite harmless.'

'A paroxysm? I see. If it's quite harmless, why does everybody in Ireland say "Bless you" when a person sneezes?'

'Don't know. It's an ancient custom, probably pagan.'

Well, what's a laugh? Is it another style of paroxysm? Let us immediately note one important distinction between the sneeze and the laugh. Human beings and animals sneeze but animals don't laugh. Maybe that's why we insist on regarding them as very thoughtful and infinitely wise. 'My slippers are missing again, as usual. That dog knows where they are. If only he could talk, he'd tell me.'

The number of things included under the head of HUMOUR is uncountable. Humour can be visual, or something written or spoken. If you have a man who has a certain arrogance of manner and who is impeccably dressed, it is very funny to pour a bucket of dirty water over him, preferably from an upstair's window. Should we not pity a person subjected to such a plight? No, indeed. We roar laughing.

Looking Back

The year 1854 did not occur yesterday. I have been looking over a bound volume of a weekly named *The*

London Journal under that date, and it seems far further away than a mere 107 years. It seems concerned with events on another planet, and the drawings which adorn it (woodcuts) look slightly unearthly. It announces itself to be a 'weekly record of literature, science and art'. I have not investigated that claim, and for a peculiar reason: I found the paper nearly impossible to read. I do not wear glasses and regard my sight as 'normal', but the print is unbelievably small. This means that the plain people had far better eyesight a century ago.

But why do I disinter this publication in the year of grace, 1961? Because it contains a funny column under the stupidly cumbrous title of FACETIAE. Is the funny stuff funny? Let the reader judge. I present samples, taken absolutely at random.

Century-Old Laughs

Benevolent Old Lady: Sakes alive, child! What do you want two pails of cold victuals for? You had only one yesterday.

Little Girl: Yes, ma'am; but mother's taken boarders since.

(I deduce here that 'cold victuals' means slops.)

Self-Possession and Presence of Mind – A thief, surprised in the act of robbing a bank, was asked what he was about; and answered, 'Only taking notes.'

Why may we reasonably expect that the Turk will succeed in preventing the Russian bear from devouring his subjects? Why, because he's a muzzle-man.

Straw is a servant that occasionally blows up its master.

An Orleans paper says: It requires three persons to start a business firm there; one to die with yellow fever, one to get killed in a duel, and the third to wind up the partnership business.

Why should money not be called 'blunt'? Because a man can 'cut a dash' with it.

We decidedly object to the first-floor lodger coming home in a state of inebriation and getting into our bed with his boots on.

When does a lady's dress resemble Joan of Arc? When it's *made of Orleans*.

The British Tar's Motto: *Semper Hide 'em*.

Cab Colloquy – First Cabby (who is run up against): Now then! Where did you pick up that old strawberry bottle you call a cab? Second Cab (retorts): Same place where yer found that bit of old rag you calls a 'orse.

A Noun of Multitude: A gentleman accustomed to the signature of the firm in which he was a partner, having to sign a baptismal register of one of his children, entered it as the son of Smith, Jones and Co.

Well, good reader, had enough? Or can you carry on a bit further? I can NOT.

Electors treated as half-wits

By the time these words come to the eye of the reader, he will find himself faced with a choice. The choice will not be whether to vote for FF or FG but whether or not to vote at all.

The election campaign has been brief (no doubt a stratagem thought clever by Mr Lemass) but it has lacked nothing of the vulgarity and brazen cheek of its many predecessors.

Both in roared open-air speeches and in garish full-page newspaper ads it is made very clear that the electors are regarded as numbskulls and half-wits.

It is assumed that he cannot tell a lie from what is at least possible as a down-to-earth reform, and accepts that men of little education are capable of making critical and far-reaching decisions on world affairs, and the domestic economy, honest dealing, and a thousand matters. There is one promise candidates will keep and, curiously, it is not one they ever make from atop a dray: I mean pocketing their handsome salaries. That is a situation one need not be too scornful about. They are professional politicians in the most absolute sense.

Sense and Senility

It is universally accepted that persons who engage in the science of government should be grown up. In practice no trust is reposed in the ancient phrase about wisdom emerging from the mouths of babes and sucklings. Yet one can reason too far in the opposite direction. Here are the ages of some FF worthies.

MacEntee	72
Ryan	69
Traynor	75
Boland	76

These are, so to speak, some of the stars. But there is no noticeable suffusion of youth elsewhere. Lemass himself is 61. Aiken is well over 63.

I lack at the moment of writing specific knowledge of the ages of FG 'shadow cabinet' but it may be assumed that they are far from being infants, even in the strict legal interpretation of that term.

It has become customary to picture Ireland as a 'young resurgent nation'. Whether or not that is true, I think it is gravely scandalous that the conduct of national affairs should be left in the hands of men in their old age. The intention of the four gentlemen I have isolated above seems to be to cling to office until they die. Let us hope that they will not live to be centenarians. Even then, they might continue to interfere in Irish political affairs from a 'safe seat' in heaven.

Small Matters

It is interesting to wonder who exactly supplies the FF and FG parties with money. (The Labour Party I cannot take seriously, since it appears to win only the votes of the disgruntled.) Not long ago an FG deputy asked the appropriate Minister to fix a minimum pork content for sausages. The Minister declined, saying that such an order 'would not be in the public interest' or words to that effect. I have long eschewed, rather than chewed, the Irish sausage because I am convinced that certain brands *contain no pork at all*! The high spice content makes it impossible for the palate to distinguish pork from horse. It must be taken that the firms benefiting from the Minister's astonishing attitude are heavy subscribers to the Party funds. The FG nose is very likely no cleaner.

The total cynicism and self-interest of both parties will make many electors other than myself wonder whether it is worth going to the trouble of voting at all.

I will not be so impertinent as to advise the reader but I do beg him to think. Some day we will have a Dáil of educated, honest men. When that day comes, an election will be important, even if candidates still scream at us when we emerge from Mass on Sundays.

Don't take leave of your senses!

For the fact is, you'd be poorly off without them. They are usually numbered as five – sight, hearing, taste, smell and touch. These faculties are operated by certain organs, under the control of the central nervous system. But man, and many other vertebrates, has not only far more senses than five but even those named are subject to an infinity of nuance and degree. Furthermore, the senses can be easily fooled.

Sight is perhaps the most important of the senses inasmuch as, apart from its own primary function, its collaboration is demanded by other senses, particularly that of taste. You can for instance, by using a perfectly harmless and tasteless dye, turn milk black. But you will have the greatest difficulty in trying to get anybody to drink it, unless you proffer the glass in pitch darkness. Nicotine is ranked as a mild narcotic and should suffice for itself. But every smoker knows that smoking a cigarette in the dark is utterly futile and unsatisfying: he cannot see the smoke.

Or consider sweets of a certain kind. They are all made from a gelatinous compound but the cunning manufacturer by using harmless dyes colours them and pretends to impart a fruit flavour; red means strawberry, dark brown is plum, very pale yellow is lemon, green is grape, and so on. The fastidious sweet-eater will pick among a bagful to find the favourite flavour. Yet they all taste absolutely alike. The eye deludes the palate that there is a difference.

On Standing Up

A sense not even hinted at in five is that of equilibrium. It is established by a labyrinth in each ear and the verifications of the sight. But even without sight, a man will always know when he is upside down, and so will many animals.

A dog or a cat held upside down will try to screw the head round to the level it would occupy if the creature were standing up. Another unscheduled sense is that of falling. You get this before you open your parachute or even when taking a high dive. Hunger and thirst are senses and can be very keen and nasty ones.

It may be said that a branch of the sense of sight is recognition. When you see something that is familiar (your lost dog, maybe) you do more than see it. And here is a curious thing about recognition-by-sight. It is a vertical faculty.

I saw a film recently which featured Burt Lancaster. This man has a strong, massive face, not unlike the side of a quarry, but you would know it anywhere. In the film he was brutally beaten up by a gang of roughs and the next scene showed him in hospital, lying on an operating table. The camera showed him in a horizontal attitude. His face (which was unmarked) was quite unrecognisable. He might as well have been Saint Peter or Santa Claus. Yet I am not quite right when I say that recognition of a face is a vertical function. Nobody would recognise the most familiar face if presented vertically but upside down.

Some Tests

How the sense of taste can be fooled if sight is withdrawn may be shown by two tests which are easily carried out, preferably in a pub. You select as the guinea-pig a man who both smokes and drinks and knows all about both occupations. First, you securely blindfold him. Then say:

'I have two cigarettes here, one lit, the other not lit. I will place a cigarette between your lips seven times successively and you are welcome to take a good pull.

After each cigarette you must say whether it was lit or not.'

It is safe to have a good bet that he will be wrong.

The other test is even more startling. Your man is still blindfolded. You buy him a bottle of Guinness and a bottle of ale. You hold a glass to his lips five times and let him have a good drink. Again, he is almost certain to fail to distinguish the one drink from the other every time.

This suggests that brewers are not to be trusted too far in the claims they make in their advertisements. I don't know. With talk of drink we are back again to that valuable thing, the sense of equilibrium.

Ah, this eve!

It would be unthinkable for anybody to write as much as a line for today's paper without acknowledging that it is Christmas. The fact cannot be ignored. Even non-Christians cannot ignore it unless they are impervious to shoves, batterings, shrill voices, and high prices for things that look very ordinary, if not useless. It is not the feast of Christmas that is in question at all but the disorder and near-panic which precedes it.

Why is the day in front of a feast-day denoted by this word 'eve'? That old servant, my dictionary, is no help here. It says bluntly that eve is short for even or evening, but adds (without giving authority) that the word is also used to denote the day preceding a Church festival.

The Church itself uses the word vigil which from the Latin means 'watch', or keeping awake in honour of the day to come. That makes sense; 'eve' doesn't.

It Can Be Wearing

It is a plain and sorry fact that as the years go on, more and more people are heard saying 'I wish it was all over,' 'I'm nearly bet,' 'Why didn't I think of buying these things two months ago?'

The chaos that is commonly known as Christmas shopping is hard to understand, since the exact date of Christmas is known a year in advance, and the prudent man or woman could obviously begin the Christmas tasks at the beginning of, say, September, take things easy, and spend such money as is available wisely, free of the distraction of crowds and hustling sales people.

If blame for the present situation is to be allotted, I fear it must be placed on the shoulders of the business community, retail and wholesale. I have a suspicion about their procedures and motives. They feel that the occasion of Christmas tends to make the majority of customers careless, sentimental and hysterical, inducing them to buy many things which the unexcited, cold, critical eye would disdain.

But suppose a wise man realises all this in time and, on the 1st of September, enters a shop and says:

'I would like to see your Christmas cards, please.'

What will happen? The lady behind the counter will look at him as if he had two heads, give a ghastly smile and beckon to the boss who is somewhere in the background. By some other gesture she will convey to him that a quare fellow has entered the premises, and to look out.

Holly is an evergreen and sprigs of it may be gathered at any time on a country walk. But no. It must be bought at the last moment from an urchin at the door, who thinks he is selling gold leaf. Absolutely everything connected with Christmas except greeting cards and perishable foodstuffs can be got all the year round if there be found a persevering pioneer who will sternly keep after what he wants. Apparently such an heroic character doesn't exist.

The Dublin Terror

An occasion which was not festive required my own presence in Dublin just a week ago. (I had to see an income tax inspector or else later face exile in Siberia.) I had to traverse almost the whole length of O'Connell Street and the experience was not very different from taking part in a needle-match on the field of international rugby. It was unnerving. Tens of thousands of young children were trailing after dishevelled mothers and hanging on to an infinity of balloons, multitudes of men reeled about with many of them the worse for drink while decent respectable men trying to hurry about their occasions got shocking falls from prams immured in the midst of the seething mobs.

It was almost impossible to make any progress, in any direction. It was common to see stout fellows from the country deciding that the way to get through lay in the use of the solid shoulder charge. Yes, CIE had made its contribution; several special trains to Dublin at excursion rates were run to convenience 'Christmas shoppers'.

Apart from bedlam and pandemonium, Dublin had absolutely nothing to offer in the way of goods that could not just as well be had, and possibly at a cheaper price, in any country town.

Well, bruised as I am, I wish all my readers a happy Christmas, but hope they will be more sensible about the one that follows.

A converted try

It takes an emergency of somewhat colossal import to prevent the holding of an international rugby match as scheduled. The last interruptions I can remember were apparently caused by the enactment of World War II. The reader should not too glibly assume that this was the most awful and disastrous war in history: let it not be overlooked that history is not yet finished.

Some cynics of recent date suggest that the Irish team is not very anxious to play, that their forward branch of the game has been very bad because they have been under the disability of having small packs. I disagree with that and believe that the boys in the green jerseys are all right provided that they have not also green faces.

And the fact is that the postponement of the Wales-Ireland encounter was due, not to small packs, but to small pocks. The usual spelling is 'smallpox', but a pock everywhere on the face is just as genuine as a puck in Croke Park.

I am an authority on smallpox and would fain recount my recent experiences. The phrase 'would fain' may seem archaic, but so am I.

March Wedding

A distant cousin insisted that I attend her wedding in Swansea on the 2nd of this month. (That means a present, I muttered to myself morosely.) In Dublin, I casually mentioned to a medical friend, though no client of his, that I would have to go.

'Tell me,' he said, 'how would you like a temperature of 104, a racing pulse, vomiting and pains all over the back and legs for a start? Then a rash that develops into a mass of pustules? Then a swelling of the head that makes your face unrecognisable and threatens death from asphyxia by blocking the air passages? And even with recovery, the certainty of being disfigured for life?'

I said I wouldn't fancy this regimen.

'Then you're a lunatic to go across without being vaccinated. Slip down to the hospital tomorrow about 11 and I'll do the little job. If I'm tied up I'll get another man to do the needful.'

'Do the needle, you mean?'

Unthinkingly, I did this. Within a week I was very ill, and in bed. In hospital.

Some Ugly Facts

Smallpox is a very painful, dangerous and largely unexplained disease, caused by a filter-passing virus, and is highly infectious. There is no settled treatment or cure for it. Emphasis of medical endeavour has been on prevention, and the very word vaccination (from L. *vacca*, a cow) was first invented in connection with the fight to control smallpox.

Following a theory of therapy now very widely distributed in use, one Dr Edward Jenner in 1798 published a paper which said, in effect, that the best way of making a man immune to smallpox was to give him smallpox.

The idea is that if he is given a minor dose of the disease, he is almost certain not to get the massive, disastrous dose. It seems to work pretty well in practice, but there are not a few quaint individuals to whom vaccination proves not only dangerous but occasionally fatal. I think I am one.

There is a disorder called vaccinia, which is really smallpox of the cow, sometimes misleadingly called cowpox. Jenner found that if a cow was infected by smallpox, the end-product of the passage of the virus through the cow's body would still be a smallpox virus but one of much diminished power and malignancy.

This, if injected in a solution of glycerine into the human arm, would cause a mild attack with the familiar pocks in a small area at the point of injection but would lack the power of causing a generalised eruption.

In 1889 a Royal Commission on vaccination was set up and in its final report of 1896, it gave approval with some reservations to the principle of vaccination against smallpox. In Britain as well as in many other countries, legislation was passed making vaccination compulsory. This led to political and social upheavals, and the inevitable appearance of 'conscientious objectors' led to some relaxation of compulsion. Responsible people have alleged and established many cases of eczema and impetigo following vaccination, and hundreds of cases of the far worse horror known as post-vaccinal encephalitis.

True, the difference in reaction of adults to vaccination is truly enormous, but it is indisputable that almost anything is better than a dose of real smallpox.

Therefore, good reader, if the next time you look over a hedge and see a cow, raise your hat.

A dreadful day

It seems, looking back, that my contributions to this newspaper have consisted mostly of my accounts of illnesses, bad luck, money owed and not paid, and every other kind of misfortune. If it's the truth, why should I be shy of telling it. The recital alone gives some relief, and might also be a sort of a warning to other people who have it in for me.

I feel the latest piece of victimisation takes some beating. For once, I will be brief about it, if only the torture was very lengthy.

One morning I got a telephone call from a television company in London. I do not disclose which company. Would I be good enough to sit for a television interview? The date suggested was a Saturday and the man speaking said that absolute quiet was essential, the place he wanted to do it in (a pub) would have to be closed.

I said certainly, though I made no comment about the pub. I knew that Irish pubs everywhere 'make' the week on Friday and Saturday, when the wage-earner drinks the wages. I did, however, as a sort of a joke ask certain proprietors if they would be good enough to close on this Saturday for a few hours, and that the television firm would pay handsome compensation. The result was the nearest thing I have seen to heart failure.

They Arrive

Yes, two bright boys came to my own house at 10.30 a.m., accompanied by three locals, very likely borrowed from Telefis. These were a camera man, a man to look after terrifying and roasting arc-lamps, and a third to attend to sound recording. All were polite enough in a bleak way, refused my hospitable offer of a drink, and went to work immediately.

I was put sitting on an upright, dining-room type of chair and No. 2 of the visitors sat near me but apparently not in the picture. The Sahara lights went on and my interlocutor (the general subject was books) began to ask me the most stupid questions imaginable.

'You shave every morning?'

'Yes.'

'What part of your face do you choose for starting shaving?'

'I have no idea.'

When the whole shot was over, No. 1 said:

'That was very . . . very . . . very good, but you raised your voice slightly when you began talking about knitting. Shall we try it again?'

And so we did, and so we did. There was no lunch because the Mammie, if I may so call her, assumed that this 10-minute orgy would last an hour or so at most. There was the added crux of making lunch for seven persons in all. I don't think we have that many chairs.

One Break

There were a few minor breaks between 'takes', and one major one. Glancing through a window, No. 1 said 'That's a nice little garden you have', went out and lay down on the grass.

'Get up, you fool,' I roared, 'that grass is wet. I don't want pneumonia on my hands as well as this television job.'

'OK,' he said, rising, 'let's try it again.'

The major break came about half an hour afterwards. The camera man had to motor into Dublin to get more film.

This outfit arrived, as I've said, at 10.30 a.m., and that's early enough for the start of any ordeal. They left at 7.30 p.m.

If any reader would like to know what this means in personal terms, let him sit on an upright chair between those hours, with no food beyond a cup of coffee, and nothing else of any kind except non-stop annoyance.

The item has not yet appeared on the TV screens, but I can certify that the recording was HELL. With knobs on.

Bad language

The title of this week's discourse need not alarm anybody, for the language throughout will be seemly. But bad language as a subject of discussion is worth while. While our dander is well down and we are at peace with the world, let us debate this question of abuse.

Every week this newspaper (like all others) has a small report about some decent, simple farmer. He has been hauled before the court for using vile and abusive language, and sometimes this is linked with the assertion that at the same time he was drunk and disorderly. Usually he is fined ten bob. And what about it? It could happen to a bishop.

Language (of any kind) is a fairly recent invention. I mean, it didn't start until about 100,000 years ago, roughly. Before that, communication – and here I include beasts as well as men – was by gesture. A hungry creature pointed to the mouth to indicate hunger.

Elephants did just the same as *homo sapiens*, except that they used the trunk instead of a finger. Hunger is one thing that precludes ambiguity. If you are hungry, you know you are suffering from hunger, irrespective of whether you are a mouse or an ostrich.

Having established the antiquity of language, the next question is – how old is bad language?

A Sorry Puzzle

It is not an easy question. The oldest documents accessible to the western world, those of Homer and Vergil, do not contain any bad language. The Book of Ardagh, edited by Dr John O'Donovan and placed as to age about AD 900, contains no obscenities or crude talk. In fact, it is mostly a biblical transcript, with wonderful and elaborate lettering. When then did man first begin to soil his mouth?

Certain pre-Christian Latinists, not the ones we were beaten up about at school, did not hesitate to be a bit dirty. Ovid was one of the bad boys and occasionally the elegant Horace could go a bit too near the edge.

Long their predecessor, Sophocles wrote a questionable play dealing with incest. A certain Dr Bowdler had to expurgate the works of Shakespeare and incidentally gave a new word to the English language. All those people seem remote, long-dead, old-fashioned.

How do we manage today, 1962, for bad language and immoral literary behaviour? I think we can boast that we are doing as well as our ancestors, but it is also true that the general public attitude for such wares has seriously declined. A dirty book is no longer an easy way of making quick money.

I haven't tried myself, but some friends of mine who know nothing about any other sort of book say that publishers have become stupid and just refuse to publish 'modern novels'. I usually offer them a cigarette and change the subject.

Our Own Man

About 40 years ago a Dublin man astonished the world (and also made it very angry) by publishing a book named *Ulysses*. His inner attitude was that there was no such thing as bad language; there was only language. It is not so much that this book was censored; my own copy bears this entry in its printing history:

'Third printing – January 1923. 500 numbered copies of which 499 seized by Customs Authorities, Folkestone.'

This statistic has always fascinated me. What happened to the 500th copy? Who has it?

It is true that *Ulysses* contains those four-letter words

but it is indeed far from being a bad book. The author was human enough to produce patches of poor and arid writing, and one large gallop of it shows that he was capable of giving himself airs by reproducing (as he thought) the styles of many writers who went before him. For all that, I believe *Ulysses* is a great book.

Its many distinctions have been imitated often enough to prove that.

Maybe that's enough to say for one week. The book is not banned in Ireland but is very hard to get. Joyce is dead and the sort of people who originally felt outraged now think the book is tame stuff. May both RIP!

Does tax hurt?

Once a year we, like our fellow-serfs on the sister-isle, are presented with a thing called the Budget. It pretends to be an annual review of the national housekeeping, looking at the economic facts of the year gone by and purporting to peer cunningly into the year that is to come. After a smug sermon lasting about an hour scolding us for our profligate and reckless habits, the elderly uncle (otherwise the Minister for Finance, whoever he may be) announces the new taxes. And that's that.

Not many people give the matter much cold, objective thought. They accept taxation and State interference with their private lives as inevitable, like death. If on the day following the day of the Budget, you ask some reasonable man what he thought of it, the response you will get is almost certain to be a sullen grunt. As a subject of conversation, the Budget is as sterile, perfunctory as the weather. All the talk in the world won't prevent the descent of a heavy shower of rain.

It is commonly and silently accepted that the main function of a government is to tax the citizens and make them as poor and insignificant as possible. To complain amounts almost to treason but most of the victims do not do this, because they realise it is a fearful waste of time. The only people who talk of taxation (and they do so with glee) are those who think they are not taxed at all. Such people do not realise that there is practically nobody in any modern community who is not taxed.

Not His Business

Let us take the case of Mr Plain Man. He has a good job, is married and has four kids. His salary is not

128

enormous but it is comfortable, and with all his allowances he pays next to nothing in income tax. He hasn't a car, of course, and doesn't go in for any nonsense of that kind. A drink? He's no TT but once a week for a few pints is enough for any man. He is sensible, shrewd, level-headed. On Budget day the Minister announces an extra duty of 3d a gallon on petrol. The PM (– stands for Plain Man, not Prime Minister) gives three cheers.

'Good enough for them,' he sniggers. 'Flashing along the roads like streaks of lightning, killing people and with a lady in the front seat who is almost certainly somebody else's wife. And plenty of drink on board, of course. Makes you sick.'

A Narrow View

A little reflection would show that this is a narrow view. A rise in the cost of petrol means a rise in the cost of distribution of everything, including essential food. It means that the cost of all goods must go up. The cost of feeding the people in the County Home goes up, and up go the rates. The Ministers, here and in Britain, pretended to make a distinction as between essential and 'luxury' goods and services. Is a newspaper a luxury? If a man thinks he badly needs a haircut, is he therefore a vain and despicable little bantam? How luxurious is it to have a hot bath now and again?

Finance Ministers all over the world believe that taking a drink or smoking a cigarette are habits which are very bad for us, and underline this decision by imposing massive taxes on those commodities. The truth is that if everybody concerned suddenly decided *en masse* to give up drinking and smoking for good, the financial foundations of the State would collapse, and new unprecedented taxes (e.g. on bread) would be necessary to enable the creaking government machine to shamble along. There is an excise tax on matches. That hits the smoker again, but what about the little wife who has to light the fire every morning?

Across the Way

Selwyn Lloyd in Britain was attacked and jeered at for putting a tax on kiddies' lollipops. The British taxpayer can well be angry at this petty impost, as with an infinity of other marginal fiscal irritations. Why? Because every now and again he is called on to pay for Britain's share in a world war when all standards of financial wisdom and equilibrium are swept completely aside, money is no object, buy X, Y and Z no matter what it costs, freedom itself is priceless, we also serve and et cetera.

It could be argued, against this background of taxation, that world wars are intermittent intervals of sanity. In Britain, World War I is not yet paid for. Two or three generations yet unborn will have to spend their days paying for Word War II. How about World War III? By then, I hope to be a recluse in Rome. Anybody who wants to get in touch with me should ring me – I know it is an old joke – at Vat 69.

Mowers to movies

This week the reader must bear with me (after all, isn't this a small bear garden we run here?) because two subjects I should like to mention have absolutely nothing to do with each other.

First of all, I got a catalogue (unsolicited) from a Dublin firm of purveyors for the needs of gardeners and small-time cultivators. The prices in it astonished me. No, not for the usual reason that they were astronomically high but because they were so low. A nice situation in 1962.

Take a lawn mower, for example. It is not a very complicated machine but it is an example of what we call precision engineering. The drum of cutting blades must have a delicately minute impact on the reactor blade against which they come. There are side effects, such as a shaft of seasoned oak, and a lubrication system which a decent half-wit could operate. What price for this small miracle? On average, a fiver!

Owner-driven

But there was more than that in this small, illustrated book. There were other mowers on offer, mechanically propelled and of unearthly appearance. The driver could ride on them, and there seems to be no reason why he should stay on lawns. There seemed to me to be no obvious reason why the owner-driver should not surge out from his modest abode of a Saturday and go to the races in the Curragh on this mower.

Compared with a taxi, the cost of a mower would be negligible and I doubt if any Guard, or even a Taca, would have the nerve to stop a contraption that looks like a cross between a mobile thermological station and a concrete mixer. The cost would be well under £40.

The Movies

Completely different is a picture I saw. On my trips to Dublin I often find myself in an elderly but smallish cinema, of which there are many similar sorts in London. You are not confronted with an epic, or a reconstruction of the most spectacular parts of the Bible story by some Hollywood mogul. You get bits and pieces – travelogues, newsreels, sometimes 'on the record' spiffs by American politicians.

You can leave when you like without feeling defrauded. There is no climax to wait for. You can rest, and even sleep. Yet, inevitably, in such tame situations, you come across positively startling material. In my case last week it was the record of a wrestling event. It was incredible, mercifully silent but with a cynical American commentator on the sound-track.

The first bout showed two tough-looking men, superb physically, trying to get the better of each other with no holds barred. It was spectacular and deadly, but not unfamiliar. Stranger things were to come.

Ladies and Gents

The next bout was between two women, one dressed in what amounted to a white bathing costume, and the other in black. There was an attempt at the same brutality, but entirely of a different kind.

The Woman in White (never mind Wilkie Collins) took her opponent by a strangle grip and slammed her to the floor on her back. While there, she took her opponent by another complicated grip and did exactly the same thing. The referee stopped this bout when the possibility of murder was nigh.

The final presentation was really unbelievable. Each corner of the ring was occupied by a superbly-built wrestler, sworn to murder the other three.

The fundamental tactic was to throw the opponent (or maybe three of them) right out of the ring among the spectators. Bashes on the face with bare fists were a commonplace, and the feet were used as often as the fists.

One could write a lot about this exposition of brutality but I am afraid that the conclusion must be that we have all enjoyed very, very rough stuff so long as other people are involved.

From Clongowes to Martello tower

Well, boys-ah-dear, there was the queer hosting at the Forty-Foot swimming hole, Sandycove, Dun Laoire, when a great number of people – perhaps 200 – gathered to honour James Joyce.

His great book *Ulysses* is very long (my own edition is in two volumes) but its events are confined to a single day and night, namely June 16, 1904; and its opening is located on the top of the Martello Tower at Sandycove where Joyce himself, Oliver St John Gogarty and an Englishman were in residence.

Ceremony?

On display in the tower itself were various relics of the master, including letters, printers' proofs and his death-mask, the last-mentioned an extremely successful cast, ironically a thing in death that was extremely life-like.

The location of Saturday's ceremony (if drinking small ones and cups of tea can be called a ceremony) afforded a curious historical conspectus. Those towers are an echo of the Napoleonic wars when the British with three ships of the line and two frigates sought with artillery to subdue a tower commanding the Gulf of San Fiorenzo.

It was only through a sheer accident – the igniting of junk on the tower which should not have been there at all – that it was eventually taken. When it was found that the tower had only two 18-pounder guns, the military lesson was obvious and was quickly learned by the British. The fear of the French invasion of the home territory was immediately provided against by the wholesale erection of the so-called Martello towers around the whole coast of England and along the eastern shores of Ireland. They are so solid and massive as to be virtually indestructible and many centuries hence will no doubt rank with our round towers as objects of speculation and wonder.

The Clongowes Boy

The wonder of Saturday's event was that it happened at all. Even ten years ago it would have been unthinkable but in more recent years the austerity and beauty of Joyce's work is finding acceptance in quarters where it had formerly won condemnation without any investigation of its worth. Even as an historical portrait not only of Dublin but of an age *Ulysses* is unique.

Joyce has left a full picture of his early self in his *Portrait of the Artist As a Young Man*, one of the finest autobiographies in the English language. To a large extent however all his writing concerns himself, his life and times. Many chance acquaintances, including people who wished him ill, have been immortalised.

Having at last shed the silly mantle of purveyor of erotica, Joyce emerges from contemporary accounts of him as a very shy man, punctilious in manner and very formal in modes of address. Sylvia Beach, an American in Paris who had the courage to publish *Ulysses* originally in 1922 and who was present on Saturday at Sandycove, an alert lady of 75, was never known or referred to by Joyce otherwise than Miss Beach.

Joyce went to school at Belvedere College and Clongowes, both institutions run by the Jesuit Fathers, and left Ireland for good at the age of 22. Left it physically, that is. His mind and memory never left Dublin. He died in 1941, during the war. Would it not be an idea to disinter the remains and rebury him at his own beloved city?

James Joyce, was born on February 2, 1882, at Rathgar and from Clongowes went to University College, Dublin, where he specialised in modern languages. He went to Paris in 1904 and for the rest of his life lived variously in France, Italy and Switzerland.

His last work, *Finnegans Wake,* is accepted as one of the most complicated and obscure pieces of writing ever to see print and if there is substance in the common belief that great mental stress and worry lead to ulcers, it is understandable that his death arose following collapse from duodenal ulcers amid the chaos of the German occupation of France.

Friends at this time urgently counselled him to go to the Irish Minister in Paris and get his British passport changed for an Irish one, for it was known that the German authorities regarded him as a British spy. He refused, saying 'it would not be honourable'.

Owed Nothing

That was another manifestation of his stiffness and formality. He certainly owed the British nothing, for they were the first to burn *Ulysses:* of 500 copies landed at Folkestone in January, 1923, the Customs Authorities seized 499.

T.S. Eliot has remarked that Joyce was the greatest master of the English language since Milton. Let us leave it at that.

My sympathies to the Carlovians

Call it delusion, hallucination, folly or just plain original sin, it is something the Irish are very prone to, though it is known all over the world: I mean this custom on the part of people who know nothing whatsoever about horse racing and who have no interest in it whereby they have a bet on a horse provided only the race is big, that is what we more knowledgeable characters call a classic.

Humdrum races at such places as Newbury, Doncaster, Mullingar or Newmarket do not count. But if the race be the Grand National or the Derby, then Mr Innocent dives into the pocket wherein he keeps the fivers. His betting, usually on a substantial scale, distorts the market and tends to annoy the regulars. And they become quite infuriated when Mr Innocent wins, as he frequently does.

Occult Method

Occasionally he tamely accepts a 'certainty' but generally he has his own mysterious methods of finding the winner – methods which are occult, arcane, or based on formulae more in keeping with the practices of the witch-doctor.

Take that affair at the Curragh. The main event was the Sweep Derby. The innocents in their regiments came forward to find the winner of this uniquely rewarding (to the horse owners) event. On the face of it, the thing was obvious.

The term Sweep Derby contains 10 letters: therefore the winner must be a horse whose name is spelt in 10 letters. This line of reasoning cuts out aberrations and distractions such as breeding, racing form, previous racing record, the 'going' and so on. It seems a godsend, an inspired short-cut; never mind if it has an odd cabalistic quality.

Only two horses in the race had names amounting to 10 letters. One was Saint Denys, ridden by the well-known P. Canty, heavily tipped in the papers and fairly heavily backed. The starting price was 100/7. Alas, it was not placed.

Outside the Rules

Perhaps, however, it was outside the rules by reason of having a name of two words. The other genuine 10-letter horse was Tambourine. Tambourine won, of course, at 10/1. The favourite Larkspur (a meagre thing of only eight letters) was 9/4, so that Tambourine's price was generous and well worthwhile.

The race was run on a Saturday, which is an eight-letter word. That gives the racecourse mystic an embarrassingly wide choice as between Larkspur, Gail Star, Borghese, Our Guile, Solpetre and Trimatic. I imagine that, finding the portents so multi-faced, he would discard all of those horses and try for another formula.

Sometimes some of the innocents back a horse because, utterly irrespective of his record or the odds, they like his name. Who would begrudge the innocents the few quid they made when Tipperary Tim won the Grand National as a total outsider at 100/1? Not I, for my father backed him and later made me a present of a toy machine-gun. I don't think there was any symbolism involved there.

Another method I have heard of is to find out on what saint's feastday the big race is to be run and then to find the horse who seems related in some way to the saint. I can't say whether such prognostication is religious, superstitious or sacrilegious; I should merely state that it is unreliable.

Now and again Mr Innocent and Mr Well-tried can become interchangeable, and I feel bold enough to sympathise with a great many Carlow people for all the money they lost last Saturday on London Gazette. This animal was bought cheaply to be set up as the object of a raffle in aid of Carlow Golf Club, whose club-house had been burnt to the ground.

Auctioned

The lady who won him put him up for auction and under his new owners and trained by Tom Jones, did really well in England. For the Sweep Derby, his jockey was confident enough to say, 'This fellow will win.' Any decent Carlowman would feel it treasonable to back any other horse, and for a local golfer it would be plain heresy. Well, starting at 33/1, he was not napped at all.

I'm afraid there is no useful conclusion to this soliloquy of mine, if it not be that most reverend old adage – 'betting on horses is worse than drink.'

Some British delusions about the Irish

The Irish people have a number of failings. So, of course, have other peoples, but it might be worthwhile glancing at those of the Irish if only to acquit them of many failings attributed to them by others which they haven't got at all.

The people who suffer most from delusions about the Irish are the British (or perhaps it would be fairer to say the English). The Englishman's attitude, I should add, however mistaken, is not hostile; in fact it is usually indulgent.

Perhaps the primary delusion of the Englishman is that the Irish spend most of their time fighting each other. Whether the fighting is done with fists or shillelaghs is not material, as no real damage is ever done.

There is no motive for these fights, no issue, nothing at stake, no *casus belli* – not even jealousy over a pretty colleen.

It was just fighting for the love of it. I believe 'trailing his coat' was a phrase originally invented in relation to the Irishman.

I note, incidentally, from many American publications that the word donnybrook (thus with a small 'd') is used in the sense of a violent row. I once lived in Donnybrook and can certify that it is a most peaceable and God-fearing district. The 'donny-' part of the word is the Gaelic *domhnach*, or church.

The Glass

The Englishman's second important belief about the Irishman is that he is always drunk. There is a shred of logic in this belief if one accepts the preceding proposition that Irishmen are also always fighting, for too much liquor can lead to blows. But there is not much sign of logic in the subordinate beliefs. Ireland is in fact a cattle-raising country and, disreputable as it may sound in theory, we have to import annually a considerable amount of wheat wherewith to make bread.

But the Englishman never sees Paddy driving, selling or owning a cow. The one animal he loves and cherishes is the pig. Not infrequently the pig lives in the house with him, rather as the Englishman himself allows his dog to dwell with him. Already the Irishman is an unusual character – drunk, fighting and having a pig in the kitchen.

How does he (and the pig, for that matter) sustain life? Both subsist on one foodstuff only – spuds. The failure of the potato crop caused the great Famine of 1845–7.

In bygone years he used to drink (in addition to potheen and lethal home-made whiskey) buttermilk but the expansion of the creamery industry and the decline of home churning – an exhausting activity carried out not by the Irishman but by his wife – has made buttermilk a rarity and the poor man deprived of it is often forced to the humiliation of having to drink pints of stout.

Aside from natural shortcomings (drunkenness, fighting) he has a multiplicity of subordinate failures. He is inordinately fond of gambling and will not hesitate to put his week's wages on a horse or even on the toss of a coin.

The fact that no money remains to buy food for his wife and family if the gamble does not come off is an afterthought and not very important.

After all, what is the relieving officer for? Or those stately palaces, the County Homes?

Well, what else is there about the Englishman's Irishman? He is dishonest. Employ him behind the counter in your public house and he will be meticulous in putting all cash into the cash register but he will quietly drink four glasses of malt every day.

If you are in business as a grocer, he will take home everything needed in the way of eatables in his own house and not a word about it. If you decide it is time for a show-down, he will listen with poorly disguised impatience to your charges and denunciation and then gently tell you he is engaged to your daughter.

All the time, no matter what he is up to, the Irishman is guilty of an abiding and usually very noticeable delinquency: he never washes himself.

He is superstitious.

He paralyses industry in Great Britain with strike after strike.

He's a Communist under the skin.

He thinks he owns and runs the United States.

All those charges, however groundless, seem to add up to one thing: the Irishman is important.

How would you define the word Celt?

It is a biggish question, I admit. Anticipating the reader, I have just reached for the dictionary and find the answer given there surprising yet oddly in pattern with what I have to say later.

Here is what the book says:

CELT – (Low Latin celtis, a chisel, a selt.) A cutting implement resembling an axe-head, made of stone or metal, found in ancient tumuli and barrows.

A wry smile may be evoked by this disclosure that a Celt is to be found in ancient barrows, as if this was the only way to get him home on Saturday nights.

It is the practice to speak of the rather short and dark-complexioned Celtic-speaking people of France, Great Britain and Ireland as Celts, although the ancient writers seem to have applied the term 'Celt' chiefly to folk of great stature, with fair hair and blue or grey eyes.

See where that leaves us? We are sort of international tramps, and we're not sure who we are.

If someone were to say, possibly by way of sneer, that one of my forebears was Brian Boru, I wouldn't be in a position to challenge the assertion.

I would probably mutter something like, 'Aw well, he fought the Danes, which is more than the Milk Marketing Board is doing today' and then shamble out, pretending I had to catch a bus. There is a lot to be said for keeping history in the schoolroom.

But recently I came across by accident a piece of literature which to some extent enlightened me, not to say shocked me.

It is a paper read before the Royal Irish Academy on 26th January last by Professor J. J. Tierney, who occupies the chair of Greek in UCD, entitled 'The

Celtic Ethnography of Posidonius' (now available in print, Hodges, Figgis & Co., Dublin, 9/–).

It would be impossible and, anyhow, unfair, to try to convey here what Professor Tierney adduces as the testimony of the ancient Posidonius. Not only does the Professor give chapter and verse but also the texts relied on.

I stumbled through page after page of Greek and then tangled with the Latin recitals (Greek is much easier to read than Latin) – only to discover, at the heel of the hunt, that English translations had been thoughtfully provided at the end.

The next section of this discourse is entirely quotation from that, and here is what Posidonius has to say about us:

The Celts sometimes engage in single combat at dinner. Assembling in arms they engage in a mock battle-drill and mutual thrust-and-parry, but sometimes wounds are inflicted and the irritation caused by this may lead even to the slaying of the opponent unless the bystanders hold them back.

And in former times when the hindquarters were served up the bravest hero took the thigh piece, and if another man claimed it they stood up and fought in single combat to the death.

The Celts sit on dried grass and have their meals served up on wooden tables raised slightly above the earth. Their food consists of a small number of loaves of bread together with a large amount of meat either boiled or roasted on charcoal or on spits.

They partake of this in a cleanly but leonine fashion, raising up whole limbs in both hands and biting off the meat, while any part of which is hard to tear off they cut through with a small dagger which hangs attached to their sword-sheath in its own scabbard.

The Celts have in their company, even in war (as well as in peace), companies whom they call parasites. These men pronounce their praises before the whole assembly and before each of the chieftains in turn as they listen. Their entertainments are called Bards. These are poets who deliver eulogies in song.

All about golfing

Well, I went along to the final on Sunday, the 22nd, of the Hospitals' Sweeps golf tournament at Woodbrook, near Bray, so narrowly won by Christy O'Connor. How sound are your nerves? How would you like £1,000 to hang on the attempt at one final putt on the last green?

I am personally no stranger to golf. Some years ago I was induced to take up the game on the course of Delgany, near Greystones, in Wicklow. On completion of 18 holes, I found myself puffed out and exhausted.

I soon gave the game up for a variety of reasons, not the least of them being the undeniable fact that all golf clubs have an enormous number of holes.

Search for Truth

My Woodbrook visit prompted me to go to reference books to find out the real facts about golf, and they turned out to be, like the Delgany course, mountainous. Many courses there are in Britain but in the United States in 1930 there were 5,691, in property value worth $830,000,000 with 2,225,000 persons playing. Today in all Ireland there are 225 courses, and a curiosity is that the Six County group does not seem to be very fond of golf.

But let's go back. The word 'golf' (in ancient times variously called goff, gouff and gowff) is said to come from the Dutch word for a club – kolf. There is a belief that the Dutch played a game not unlike golf except that they did it on ice, and that the Scots copied the idea. The widely-held notion that modern golf originated in Scotland may yet be the answer to your blazing Irish hothead who roars about golf being a 'foreign game'. Everybody knows that Ireland invented Scotland and gave her her original language.

The first Scotch reference to the game is in a decree of parliament dated 1457 which ordains, as to Sunday, that 'the futeball and golf be utterly cryit down, and nocht usit.' The original concern about the cult of golf was that it led to neglect of the important science of archery.

In 1491 an angry decree read: 'Futeball and Golfe forbidden – item, it is statut and ordainit that in na place of the realme there be usit futeball, golfe or uther sik unprofitabill sportis.' But royal taste changed.

In 1603 James VI (later James I of England) appointed one William Mayme to 'during all the dayes of his lyif-tyme, club-maker to his Hienes.' It was those and similar utterances that caused golf to be known as the 'royal and ancient' game, and the foundation at St Andrews of the club with that name which has become the governing body of golf in this hemisphere.

It would be tedious to trace progress from primitive to modern golf. Even the golfball has its private history. Up to 1848 the ball was of leather, stuffed with 'as many feathers as a hat will hold'. They were easily battered out of shape and were of no use in wet weather.

There was great welcome for the 'guttie' ball which followed, made from solid gutta-percha, but this was liable to break up into tiny pieces. The modern rubber-cored ball was invented by an American in 1898. The official US ball is larger than that of Europe.

Players? There have been many famous ones, and still remembered (and still alive at a pleasant age of 60) is Bobbie Jones, an amateur who had his first sensational win in 1916 and who in 1930 made a clean sweep of the world's most difficult targets – the British Amateur and Open and the US Amateur and Open.

How his skill would compare with today's magicians' is another question. The top professional in the US in 1921 was Walter Hagen. In the two following years he was succeeded by Gene Sarazen but Hagen was again top in the four years 1924–7.

I noticed that the US took the Great War so seriously that there was no competition in 1917–18.

But here is the ultimate statistic that will make many golfers angrily shout 'Liar!' The diameter of the hole on the green is FOUR AND A HALF INCHES.

Man in the street

Today in Britain and to a somewhat lesser extent here, much attention is being showered on that eternal wayfarer, the Man in the Street.

For years there has been an Institute of British Standards which lays down the specification, size, weight and function of various articles.

Other bodies prescribe the content of sundry manufactured items of food and drink, and even the strength to which some of them must conform, as e.g. whiskey.

From the Cow

Milk is minutely supervised from the point when it leaves the cow till it arrives in a sterilised bottle on the citizen's doorstep, and frequently prosecutions for deficiency or adulteration are proof that those in authority do not lack vigilance.

Despite occasional and alarming breakdowns such as the recent scare about the drug thalidomide, there is strict surveillance of the production of drugs, narcotics and pharmaceutical products.

Most proprietary products must bear on the label a statement of the chemicals and the amount of them contained in a particular product, and the law insists that many things which doctors enjoin us to take for our various ailments must be labelled Poison.

Yet this complicated and intricate apparatus for making sure that the customer is not only right but all right is indeed far from perfect; there are cracks and fissures and even chasms, and many an operator who is not only able but also unscrupulous can wangle many a questionable substance through the net.

Under our own last Health Act elaborate regulations

apply to the storage, handling and exposure for sale of foodstuffs but it is common knowledge that in many shops little or no attention is paid to them.

Indeed, enforcement, inspection and sampling is in itself a formidable task. Recently in Britain a new body has been set up to attend to misleading, exaggerated or downright fraudulent advertising, but many members of the public are by no means convinced that the move will achieve any spectacular improvement.

Every particular make of 16 different makes of motor car is still easily the best of the lot. There is only one decent holiday resort in all Ireland, one newspaper, one golf course, one hotel, one make of shirt.

I have an old cutting (alas, undated) from the London *Daily Telegraph* dealing with some observations made by the Public Analyst for the City of London at a meeting of the Royal Society of Health. Here were some of his disclosures:

The meringue, formerly composed of white of egg and sugar, was now made from an 'artificial cellulose gum in place of the egg'.

Among products debased in one way or another were beer, cordials, custards, jam, demerara sugar, mustard, French coffee, shortbread, lemon curd and some of the more expensive teas.

What is presented as 'whipped' or 'Jersey' cream often is of a grade of cream containing less fat than was usual in plain cream before the last war. What is often put forward as pâté de foie has nothing to do with the livers of geese.

'Meat pies' were an amalgam of meat and potato. Cider was sweetened with saccharin, fish paste contained as little as 25 per cent of the fish specified.

Apart from the unannounced use of substitutes and adulteration in general, there had been many prosecutions for the finding of foreign bodies in food and the sale of food that was mouldy, maggoty, unfit or rancid.

The wonder is that some of us are alive at all.

The problem is so big and wide that it is very difficult

and in some respects intractable. What can one do if one finds bugs in one's hotel bed?

Write to Bord Fáilte, certainly, but will that cure the bites? A good safeguard against thirst is to have a syphon of lemonade in the house; it is a good refreshing drink but it has nothing whatever to do with lemons.

It is merely tap-water charged with carbonic acid gas and flavoured with some chemical. A great number of other 'fruit' drinks and even confectionery have absolutely no fruit content.

Every individual has his or her own pet complaint adulteration and deficiency in a particular thing. My own, I am sure, will be echoed by many males.

Yellow Pockets

When I was much younger the pockets in the trousers of even the cheapest suit were made of yellow, indestructible canvas. They were the pockets of the greatest stress, containing not only weighty metal things like coins and keys but also too often a heavy pair of hands.

Nowadays the pockets of even an expensive suit are made apparently of cotton, sure to be riddled with holes after a month's wear.

I suppose it's one argument for going back to the kilt and sporran.

Knowall on the weather

Well, there you are and where are you? The first time I read that phrase I thought it was profoundly wise, subtle and terribly true. But after some weeks reflecting on it, I decided it was quite meaningless and just damn silly.

But now I'm not so sure. It does seem to have a queer psychic import. It bears nothing so simple as an actual meaning but a sinister suggestion, a warning, a threat of the necessity of taking care.

There is almost a hint of nuclear disaster just around the corner, germ warfare perhaps, or generalised rheumatism of the brain. After all, this is 1963 and the world is bound to get worse before it's better.

Ireland has had at least four days of snow and frost. A nationwide epidemic of leprosy could not have shaken the country more. Thunderous news reports on the radio gave ever more fearful details of the momentous crisis.

Two men were starving to death in a cottage at Ticknock, County Dublin, and the question of requisitioning a Constellation of Irish Airline was under consideration; the dropping of four loaves of bread was planned but nobody could be sure whether it was brown bread or white bread they liked.

A banshee had fainted from the cold on the border of county Carlow. A hop-off-my-thumb from Strabane had savagely assaulted a B. Special with an icicle which contained plaster of Paris. In Ballymore Eustace an old man demented with chilblains mistook a bag of coal for tobacco and had smoked three pipefuls of it before he could be stopped.

Nobody doubts that the heart of Ireland is sound but if everybody in the country was to be frozen to death, what then?

In the middle of all this terrible consternation a Dublin paper made editorially and very casually a revelation which startled the few people who had retained the use of cold reason.

That Government committee, the paper said, had been sitting for four months and had not yet reported. That was not good enough. If it could not bring its deliberations to an early close and make a recommendation, the Government should ignore it and go ahead within the confines of its own judgement.

The time for action had come; mere talk had rarely solved any problem of grave national importance. There was indeed far too much talk in this country.

Know what this committee was pondering for so long?

That the State here should buy one helicopter!

At the present time there is absolutely no helicopter anywhere in the 26 counties.

True, disasters at sea threatening along our very extended coastline call for rescue intervention by helicopter and with no shyness at all our respectable Government alerts the British Navy at Derry, who usually have already despatched a machine on its errand of mercy and hope.

It seems that in Ireland the British are now accepted as the haven of last resort. We would be lost without them.

What does a helicopter cost?

Personally I have no idea but a knowledgeable friend tells me that the standard machine can be got for about £50,000, and that maintenance costs are nominal.

This sum of £50,000 is, of course, enormous but one should remember that our prodigiously numerous collection of Ministers and Parliamentary Secretaries are fluthering about the place in brand-new cars of the Mercedes Benz make; those cars are good but they are not cheap.

Some people feel (and I am one of them) that a second-hand Post Office bike would be the very man for this job, and more in keeping with the ancestry of our betters. For that reason one may take it as the general feeling that one helicopter for the whole country would be preferable to having innocent people drowned or frozen to death.

From another point of view, £50,000 is not really so much if one finds oneself in this new dimension we call air travel, for there costs tend to take on a fictional quality and the tendency is to ignore them.

What does money matter if the question is one of prestige and national pride, to say nothing of convenience and safeguarding life? Aer Lingus (Irish Air Lines) have three Constellation aircraft.

Know what they cost? One million pounds each, with goodness knows what maintenance burden. I suppose it's all right, since those giant birds stimulate emigration and also bring American tourists here to be skinned alive.

Meantime, I have chilblains on my corns. Any reader who knows of a remedy will be sent a book token value three shillings.

The power of darkness

The observant wayfarer in this vale of tears will have noticed that misfortunes do not come singly. They more usually descend in a shower.

Since about Thursday night, the 10th January practically everybody I know (including myself) has been in a bad temper. Although Cuba is far away, perhaps this countrywide depression dates from that very narrow shave the whole human race had.

As I write these lines, news has come over the electric radio of the death of Hugh Gaitskell, one of the brilliant and academically distinguished lights of the Labour Party in Britain. Western Europe can ill afford such a loss at this stage of tumult and threat. The Congo situation, though apparently nearing a stage of finality, due mostly to exhaustion of the militant natives of Katanga, was never a very pleasing operation and one feels that if there is to be a truce, it will be an armed truce.

But most of the continent of Africa is unsettled and unhappy, not the least part of it being South Africa, where the minority whites have indulged in the most cynical exacerbation of relations with the natives.

Then there is universal puzzlement about the entry of ourselves (with Britain) into the Common Market. Such comment as has been forthcoming from official sources is vague in the extreme but generally admits that native industries long sheltered by a tariff wall will be wiped out. It is also admitted that the price of food here will go up, and that there will be a general rise in the cost of living.

Unemployment and dearer food are not enticements, and could result in steeper emigration figures. Some people have assured us that membership of the Common Market will automatically make the existence of the Six Counties as part of the United Kingdom a meaningless anachronism. In other words there is a fearful amount of guesswork and prophecy going on. I am personally too cunning to contribute my share here.

But nobody writing on the subject of contemporary hardship, local and international, can dodge comment on the main excruciation: I mean the awful descent of snow and frost. It has meant, sometimes absolutely literally, just paralysis. If this country, with its natural wealth of food and fuel, collapses at the onset of a week of stern weather, what would happen if there came from the skies not snow but several thousand armed invaders, aimed by aircraft at strategic points such as big towns, rail centres, water reservoirs and installations for the production of electricity?

It is a sobering subject for meditation, for the truth is that there is no pre-arranged apparatus in the country to deal with a short period of very severe weather. Those who have listened to radio news from Britain console themselves with the thought that what the British are getting is something far worse, with the situation made more bitter in the eastern district, including London, by the coinciding go-slow of workers in the power stations.

Tough phrases like 'national sabotage' have been used to describe this semi-strike activity, condemned as roundly by the unions as by the Government and the newspapers. It certainly imparts one lesson that should be learnt everywhere, and that is the utter dependence of modern human living on the supply of current artificially generated.

Theatres, cinemas, streets, phones and electric razors can all be reduced within a few hours to chaos and nullity.

Reports seem agreed that Dublin, Wicklow and Waterford got the worst dose of snow and ice but to show there was no purely geographical rancour, Donegal was also refrigerated. In Wicklow there were situations reported which for exaggeration seemed to border on the comic.

In one remote cottage one old man who lived alone survived, fireless, for ten days on turnips, presumably eaten raw. Another man who died could not be buried or even taken out of his house. A Dublin evening newspaper, never reluctant to adopt the heroic role, hired an aeroplane to drop parcels on Wicklow farmsteads.

Unfortunately it printed a picture of the plane in flight, and it was a *biplane*. Like many people, I did not think there was any such machine now in existence and wondered who had been so carefully hiding a fighter of World War I? Many people also wondered exactly what was in those parcels? Eight sods of turf, two loaves of bread, a quarter lb of butter, two ounces of tea and 20 cigarettes – but no matches?

Mystery abounds. Surely an isolated cottier in wild mountain country has a rick of turf outside his door? He must also (one thinks) have a supply of at least a month of tea, flour to bake bread, a pound of rashers, maybe a bit of gur cake, and a big bit of plug tobacco for his pipe. Indeed, nowadays it is nearly certain that he also has a television set, and his wife and sons are probably there to make possible a hand of cards.

If any general conclusion is possible, it must be that we Irish are getting soft. How could we be getting soft, a famished farmer may roar, when me boots is frozen solid and the well where I get me water is frizen? I won't attempt to answer. Engendering heat in print won't make my own yield water. I pray tonight for a thaw, when all my pipes will burst, damaging carpets and ruining wallpaper.

No work past fifty

What are your Best Years, capital letters and all? I will try to explain. Recently I came across a paperback with the challenging title *How to Enjoy Retirement*, by Walter B. Pitkin (Cedar Books, 2/6) and, though evidently intended as a serious treatise however brightly written, I found parts of it amusing and other parts of it replete with what seemed plain ignorance.

An initial shock was the discovery that the assumed age for retirement is 50, which is sometimes in Ireland the age at which an earnest worker gets his first promotion or rise. Some probing about revealed that Mr Pitkin is an American, that his admonitions are primarily addressed to other Americans and that he is also the author of another book named *Life Begins at Forty*.

In the *Retirement* he deduces enormous possibilities from what he calls the arrival of the 'Atomic Age' but never mentions the chance that nuclear science could lead to the extermination of the human race. The form of uranium known as U235 could produce rays so powerful as practically to abolish disease.

If you are now thirty or so, he says, 'women will finish with child-bearing in their mid-twenties, children will learn how to shift for themselves around sixteen. Parents will be on their own soon after forty, with the wide, wide world ahead of them and everywhere to go.' One can only reflect that people of that kind must have been mighty precocious.

If the mother had 4 children she must have been married at perhaps 17. If those children were considered to be on their own at 16, they could have had little more than an elementary education, and the father (just like those children) must have collared a fat job with no qualifications for it, to support such a household, having married at 18.

How did he save the money to travel the wide, wide world with his wife when both were just over forty? He solves this simply by saying that twelve shillings out of every pound are in the pockets or the banks of people over fifty.

In regard to health, he mentions countless revolutionary discoveries of the Atomic Age, many still top-secret. Fourteen years ago, he asks, who had heard of penicillin ... or curare?

I would reply that the curative principle of penicillin has been known for centuries in rural Ireland, usually associated with cow-dung which has been some time lying in the field. Curare? It was in use by the Indians of Southern America even in primitive times.

But don't worry. He says that the Russians have completely cured tens of thousands of people with a new serum they have developed. What's more, influenza is no trouble, for doctors everywhere are using a vaccine which abolishes it. Can peptic ulcers be cured without drugs or an operation? Of course. The correct treatment is now routine.

Of cancer (the top killing disease in Ireland for a long, long time) he says that now most cases can be wholly cured or alleviated if caught early. Arthritis is a fairly common affliction which can be so deadly as to amount to paralysis.

It would be tedious to pursue Mr Pitkin further in his role of therapist but perhaps it is worth mentioning his view concerning the ice-cap of Greenland.

This ice-cap could be easily melted by atom bombs, and geophysicists have testified that the ice would never return there. The result of this operation would be startling, according to our author.

'England would bask under the sun of Seville, while the Scots would give up oatmeal and go in for home-made orange juice.' But he is wary here and counsels against atom-bombing the ice-fields of Antarctica.

Such a move would release so much new water that

great London and Calcutta would be submerged to a depth of 150 feet of blue water.

But what are his positive recommendations for attaining and spending the Best Years? After passing forty, he should start a tapering-off process to get mind and body gradually attuned to the condition of doing no work.

Naturally there is any amount of money laid by in the bank but an abrupt stoppage of work at 50 would be a very serious mistake, possibly fatal.

He should start 'vacating' from his office several times a year. (For most of us people here, that would be just not going to work and would mean the sack.) But for the retiring American, this procedure would make other members of the firm get used to the idea that he was not indispensable.

As the years went by he would step up this procedure by going in to work only three or perhaps two days a week. On attaining fifty and on the brink of enjoying the Best Years, he would be practically non-existent as a worker.

After that, his life is generously left to his own personal inclinations. A tour of the wide, wide world and a dumb stare at the Taj Mahal? Certainly. By all means he should read books, though think twice about trying to write them.

Woodworking (but with power tools) is a grand way of spending post-50 days, and so is golf in strict moderation. Home-made movies, membership of useful clubs and philanthropic activities can be absorbing. And so on.

I don't think this book is convincing anywhere. It was written in 1947, when presumably Mr Pitkin had reached the Best Years himself, and that would make him today at least 80. I wonder is the gentleman still alive?

To hang or not to hang

There was curiously little public interest or comment when it was recently announced in the Dáil that the Government would shortly take steps to abolish capital punishment 'except in certain cases'.

In fact we are one of the few sovereign civilised states west of the Curtain to retain it. Leaving aside time of war and martial law, it has not existed in Austria since 1918, Belgium 1873, Finland 1889, Holland 1870, Norway 1875, Portugal 1886, Spain 1932, Switzerland 1874, New Zealand 1941.

It has been abolished (with certain qualifications) in all the republics of Latin America. Curiously, however, it has been abolished in only six of the United States, the others variously prescribing hanging, the choice of shooting or hanging, and electrocution.

Arguments

It is to be hoped that we will not have in Ireland when the matter comes to legislation a re-recital of all the tedious arguments pro and con the decision. We are entitled to rely on the experience of countries which have been long without this penalty and to decide, its barbarity apart, whether its retention in the statute book acts as a deterrent upon the criminal-minded.

All the figures prove that it does not. The usual explanation for this result is that in practice very few murders are premeditated, and in the temper and passion which dominate the committing of the foul deed in other cases, no penalty can overshadow the moment of crisis.

But treason, it may be remarked, is another matter, It can be argued that the culprit who is shown to have menaced not an individual but a whole community must be put condignly to death, if only as the most effective form of warning to others.

Within the longest memory Ireland has never had a native hangman. Many years ago the present writer entered Fanning's public house in Lincoln Place, Dublin (Oliver Gogarty's 'Indignation House'), just to have a quiet, solitary drink.

Present at the counter however was an elderly, low-sized, darkly dressed gentleman complete with bowler hat. A staid family solicitor, perhaps. He was accompanied by a much younger man. After casual salutation we got talking and it was not long until I realised that my new acquaintance was Pierpoint, the public executioner, over here to do 'a job'.

His predecessor Ellis, I recall, had committed suicide. His young companion was a nephew who was learning the trade and, I was told, 'another few necks and 'e'll be ole reight.'

While dealing appreciatively with a pint of stout, Pierpoint without any shyness said that the fee he got for a 'job' in Dublin was ten guineas plus generous travelling and subsistence allowance, the latter expenses also extending to the nephew.

On one occasion our parsimonious and incredibly tactless Department of Finance tried to tell Pierpoint that there had been a reprieve at the last minute and in the circumstances expenses only would be payable. Apparently the flare-up which followed was momentous.

The hangman pointed out that it was not he who had granted the reprieve, that he would sue the Irish Government for breach of contract, and that he would never come here for another 'job' again. The Department quickly paid up, for a public court hearing on such an issue was unthinkable.

Pierpoint told me that he personally did not accept the widely believed and indeed propagated view that death by hanging was instantaneous through fracture of the spinal column by reason of the 'drop'. Many men he had hanged had shown many signs of life for up to ten minutes after the launch into eternity.

20 Minutes

It is scarcely possible for anybody to be sure that such signs are not merely post-mortem reflexes of the physical apparatus but it is a fact that the hanged man is not cut down until at least twenty minutes have elapsed.

One of the results of the descent of Roy Thomson on Fleet Street, London, was the disappearance of the *Sunday Dispatch,* originally the *Weekly Dispatch.*

In 1850 Charles Dickens wrote to the Editor protesting against the shocking scenes he had witnessed at the public hanging of a Mr and Mrs Manning for shooting dead one Patrick O'Connor for his money. Extracts:

'As the night went on, screeching and laughing and yelling in strong chorus of parodies on negro melodies, with substitutes of "Mrs Manning" for "Susannah" and the like, were added to these. When the day dawned thieves, low prostitutes, ruffians and vagabonds of every kind flocked on to the ground, with every variety of offensive and foul behaviour.

'Fightings, faintings, whistlings, imitations of Punch, brutal jokes, tumultuous demonstrations of indecent delight when swooning women were dragged out of the crowd by the police with their dresses disordered gave a new zest to the general entertainment...

'When the two miserable creatures who attracted all this ghastly sight about them were turned quivering into the air, there was no more emotion, no more pity, no more judgement, no more restraint in any of the previous obscenities than if the name of Christ had never been heard in this world...'

Public hangings in England did not cease until 1868.

Firmness about farms

Much credit must be granted, not only in mart and tavern but also at the bank, to this newspaper for last week's supplement on agriculture. Yet – need I say it? – not the theme but the attitude fills me with disquiet.

Is agriculture creditable or is its pursuit defensible at all? Maybe I read too many foreign papers and magazines to claim an impartial adjudication on those conundrums but if I were in good form (which please God I will be after Easter) I believe I could pile up a fearsome mountain of anti-agriculture facts. This week I mean merely to toy with the subject.

First, agriculture is alien and un-Irish. Cultivating the soil was never part of Irish heritage. Visually, the conspect of the older Ireland was forest, shoulders of mountain, bog and intervals of grassland pasturage. The fundamental of diet was hunting and domestic cultivation of livestock including deer. Grain crops were unknown.

Poetry may seem a very tenuous link in the formulation of social history but in all of the mass of it I have studied in the past, there is no mention in the period that is material to these notes (say 1500–1750) of cultivation or grain crops.

Bread is hardly ever mentioned and the one plant which was the cause of the country's greatest single disaster – the potato – had never been heard of. Notwithstanding that it is clear enough that certain grains had been imported in small quantities and that a lord might produce bread with the same air as a lordling of today who would produce truffles from Normandy; bread was un-Irish.

And liquor? There is ample evidence that the potheen-maker was as active in past centuries as he is inextinctible today, but the Irish gentry drank wine when they could get their hands on it. Their link with the continent was not only venal but vinous. The French were nearly always in the bay.

But let us not dwell in the past – avoid the present as much as possible also and look to the future. For a long time one of the least appetising things piled on President Kennedy's plate in the US has been agriculture.

In the great prairie sectors of that continent even the farmers have votes and they must in the political interest be treated carefully and kindly. For many years a fabulous system of farm price-support has been in operation in the US whereby there has been an induced production of foodstuffs – mostly grain – in bulk, many hundreds of times more than the US people could consume.

Apart from the cruel drain on public funds, with the taxpayer inarticulate with rage, the mere storage of grain has been a considerable technical and financial problem, and even a policy of 'take-it-away-for-nothing' has proved to be a very costly recourse by the State.

Tens of thousands of tons have been shovelled buckshee to Germany, Poland, some Scandinavian intake points, South America and even *sub rosa* via Hong Kong to Communist China. The US has found that growing more than a little food is a dead loss.

Little Ireland has today a population totally less than half of greater London. One is staggered to reflect on how, say, milk is got every day to the inhabitants of that city, how, where and when bread is baked to feed them, and with what.

The human intellect boggles at such tasks with the Fathers at Dalgan Park, rather than face up to them. Yet one of the kingpieces of our economy here is the cattle trade.

Many people – including members of the Government – seem to think that it is a proud boast that we find our tiny motherland spacious enough to breed and fatten cows to grace British tables, no matter if our native herds of humans have to emigrate to get anything as nourishing as the life the bullocks get here.

It will take a great shock, caused possibly by use of dynamite, to blast away my conviction that agriculture is a slave occupation. A greater detonation (– hydrogen bombs?) may be necessary to blast away the same conviction from the country people. Why do so many people born to the land want to leave the country and start elsewhere making motor cars?

With its surplus wheat the United States could feed this country many times over without feeling anything out of the way had been done. Meantime at Shannon Airport a considerable enterprise in precision manufacturers has been developed, the nucleus of the sort of national activity that has made the little Netherlands formidable counters in the industrial free-for-all of today's Europe.

It sounds pathetic and to some even offensive, but could Paddy not grow up? Give his pig a skelp and tell it to get out of his sight? Use his intelligence?

Don't say yes – say maybe!

When invited to do something that looks easy and appears even pleasant enough in prospect, as well as financially rewarding, the best thing is to say that you'll think about it rather than say YES straight out. That's the sort of thinking I'm doing here this week.

A Very Important Person asked me would I write an article, one of a series by other persons as distinguished as myself, and all treating of the same theme? The theme was 'The First Book I Ever Read'.

Yes, it looks easy. But is it? Ponder it for a minute and you will possibly agree that it is not easy at all. Taken seriously, it may be impossible. It may even be in the same category as would be the theme 'The Last Book I Shall Ever Read'.

In the ordinary meaning of the word, history is a vast and complicated panorama of man's existence on this planet through the countless ages, his doings, his glorious achievements and his collapses in torrents of blood.

History embraces even the development of the human mind, the attempts of reason to grapple with the mysterious and hidden nature of the universe, the immense minuteness of the Creation, and the task of locating and knowing God.

Indeed, the concept of history is more than any one human head can contain, and this will be plain enough to any man who tries to confine his study to the history of his own individual self. Just try it, and see how often you will be pulled up by faults of memory and record and by many inexplicable confusions.

For instance, nobody can remember being born. That is easy, you may say, I know my birthday and can get my State birth certificate from the Register-General for three shillings and sixpence. Well, perhaps. But things were not always thus.

It is only within the last 25 years or so that persons otherwise qualified could automatically get the old age pension. Before that an applicant had great difficulty in establishing that he had reached the age of 70 because compulsory notification of birth, marriage and death did not exist at the time he was born; baptismal records where they survived sometimes helped, as did the testimony of other grand old neighbours.

Leaving milk aside, who could write an account of the first meal he ate? Theologists hold that a normal person attains the use of reason between the age of 7 and 8, and memory, as a rational process, can scarcely be said to be functioning before that age. True, most of us have glimpses of things which happened or things we did as babies, but they are fleeting inchoate visions, quite unreliable; some of them may be fancies, or even dreams.

But leaving childhood aside, it is notorious that some of us have very bad memories at the best of times, and I'm not hinting at that ten-bob note that was never returned. Most male adults of today take a drink. How many of them remember the time and occasion of their first pint? Curiously, I can do so. I think it is because there was a pub across the road from where I went to school and at lunch-break one day a fellow student gave me an invitation (which I took as a challenge) to hop across the road with him and have one. It was strong plain porter and cost sevenpence.

But countless other important and even momentous milestones are unmarked in memory's record. When did you have your first smoke, for instance? What was the date of that disaster that was to condemn you to years of coughing, spitting and reckless waste of money? Bitterly let us confess we cannot tell.

When did you discard short pants for long trousers and how did this sharp step from boy to man feel at the time? Shaving, too – when did that begin? Most boys owned a bicycle, but when did the first one arrive? Or how about learning to drive a car?

Before attempting that 'First Book I Ever Read' I should like to see the accounts given by some of the other persons invited. I feel a fair sprinkling of humbugs and hypocrites would be bound to emerge. Very likely some smug fellow would calmly say that the first book he ever read was the first Book of Homer's *Iliad* (though I think the title of the theme excludes school books). Another high-minded character might claim that the first book he ever read was the Penny Catechism – which now costs, I am told, one and three. And some wily smart-alec might distort the theme and write about the first book he ever made, being even in earliest youth very interested in the ponies.

My own reluctant conclusion is that the thing is impossible, if one is to be honest and factual. It would be easier and at least possible to write about the first book one remembers having read, the first book which stuck in the mind. And I would say that for anybody in my own age group, the book would most certainly be one by Charles Dickens, though by no means to be ignored is the possibility that it was 'Knocknagow'.

Where's the nigger
in this woodpile?

Every ever-so-often I present here a dissertation on the meaning and usage of words; this pleases some people and infuriates others, who think words are arid and dessicated playthings but the subject is really important since words are the only tools we have for conveying anything but the simplest and plainest meaning.

Consider first the trick of intonation we call accent. By any standard of measurement Ireland is a tiny country, yet the northern and southern accents are totally dissimilar, and so is the pronunciation. The slow drawl that is heard in Tyrone is in great contrast with the sharp, rifle-crack parlance of Cork. Why should this be, and what causes this considerable variation? Personally I do not know. It cannot be topography, for landscape north and south is largely the same; there is a small possibility that the reason may be racial, though passing time should long have effaced that. In Britain the situation is far worse for, though the language is the same, people in the far north do not understand a word the southerners are saying.

I have been brooding on the great number of words in English which have totally different meanings as between Europe and the USA. Take the motor car, which is still nearly always an automobile in the States. With us the hood is that deplorable canvas affair to be erected or taken down with unmanageable arms; there it means our bonnet. (But hood is also short for hoodlum, or gangster.) Where we have a gear lever, they have a shift. When they need a refreshing milk shake or a bag of sweets (candy) they go to, of all places, a drug store. With us hardware could mean anything from barbed wire to buckets but this is the word they have for tanks and artillery. We go up in a lift but they insist on using the elevator. London has an underground system while

New York has a subway and an entertainment which is a movie there becomes a picture or a film over here. An American vagrant is a bum but with us the word has quite another meaning. A most important difference attaches to the meaning of billion; here it means a million million, there a mere thousand million.

Mention of movies should remind us that the Americans have dozens of words or locutions which cannot properly be classed as slang but for which we have no native equivalent word at all. Just try translating the following:

Gatecrasher, flophouse, make a getaway, rough-house racketeer, lounge-lizard, OK, snap out of it, live wire, hard-boiled, down and out, go-getter, guy, pan out, pussyfoot, played out, quitter, size up, bawl out, canned music, cinch, double cross, bring home the bacon, monkey business, get down to brass tacks, sugar daddy, speakeasy, fourflusher, jinx, on the spot.

When it comes to slang proper, the sky's the limit (which is itself a bit of slang). A rubberneck is a person who gawks stupidly at things, a rube is a country bumpkin, a man who commits suicide takes the Dutch route. A car which has much ostentatious ornamentation has pizzaz and when the presentation of a play is deliberately inflated and exaggerated, what has happened is a case of lollapalooza. And so on ad infinitum.

Conversely, the British have many words of their own which would puzzle even smart Americans. Samples which come to mind are biff, humdinger, conchy (– note here that the military abbreviation CO can mean either conscientious objector or commanding officer), scrounge, cushy, fag, iron rations, copper, jabber, rung, pug, tippler, peepers, clink, cove.

A nigger in the woodpile is another bit of slang, but can you find him? In the first paragraph a fairly commonplace plain English word is very badly misspelled. No prize is offered, but can you find it? I would nearly bet you cannot, even if you look over my prose again several times. The answer is upside down here below.

ANSWER

The word is desiccated. It is based on the Latin word siccus, meaning 'dry'.

Old troubles of a newspaper

Strikes, threats of redundancy, fears of disemployment through automation and other labour troubles are accepted as normal features of our time. Our bus strike has caused national chaos and severe public hardship; it is only a fortnight ago that a settlement was reached in a strike of all New York newspapers which left the citizens without any paper for 114 days; and everybody agreed that radio news was no substitute.

But let nobody suppose that such goings-on are characteristic of the second half of the twentieth century. I present this week some notes on the history of that august organ *The Times* of London.

It was started in 1785 by a John Walter but under the name of the *Daily Universal Register*; he changed the title to *The Times* on the 1st January, 1788, and was in the habit of calling his publication 'a logographic newspaper'. That term would probably puzzle the printers of today but it proves that Walter was a very intelligent and far-seeing man.

Of course type was set by hand in those days but the logographic system, for which Walter held several patents, entailed casting all the more frequently recurring words in one piece, entire. It was in fact a system of partial stereotyping. It was said by the wits that his orders to the type-founders ran like this: 'Send me a hundredweight, in separate pounds, of *heat, cold, wet, dry, murder, fire, dreadful robbery, atrocious outrage, fearful calamity* and *alarming explosion.*'

Being an Editor in those days was no honour and no joke. In a climate of political storm Walter was imprisoned several times for articles against important people and in 1790 had to stand in the pillory for a libel against the Duke of York. He died in 1812 and his son who succeeded him was the real founder of the paper's greatness and reputation. But he also offended the Government and they retaliated in a way unfortunately familiar to newspapers of today – they withdrew their standing order for the printing of lists of Customs duties and all their advertising. In those days there were no book reviews but great attention was paid to the drama.

And now along comes that most contentious thing we call progress. *The Times* had been laboriously printed by hand-press, several pressmen struggling for hours to produce the 4,000 or so copies which was the total circulation. A compositor named Martyn had invented a machine superseding this method and which was powered by steam.

The pressmen threatened to wreck this machine if it was installed but it was smuggled into the office piecemeal, with Walter going about under various disguises lest the workmen set about wrecking him personally. His courage failed when the moment for action arrived but he returned to the charge in 1814, when he had the mechanical plant installed in the house next door to *The Times* office.

One night he entered the old pressroom with a copy of this paper, the ink still wet, in his hand and told the pressmen to their astonishment, that the paper had just been printed by steam. He added that if they tried any rough stuff, he had already arranged to have all the protection he needed at hand, and that every man would continue to receive his pay until new employment was found for him. There was something eerily modern about that 'no redundancy' tactic.

That machine was too complicated, however, and another firm invented the cylindrical method of printing as known today, with a speed of 8,000 copies an hour. Then came Hoe's process, with speeds of up to 22,000 copies.

The Times had been nicknamed 'The Thunderer' by Carlisle, and many Irishmen were associated with it, as they still are. An Irishman named Captain Stirling, who had fought in the battle of Vinegar Hill (I am sorry I cannot say on which side) was paid over £2,000 a year for writing ferocious leading articles.

Tom Moore was offered £100 a month if he would contribute, and Southey turned down an offer of £2,000 a year if he would take over the editorial chair. John Delane, who retired through ill-health in 1877, was the paper's most competent and distinguished editor since the start and gave it the final polish that won it worldwide respect and esteem.

Yet in those early days the paper lacked the dignity (which some people would call smugness) which informs it today. It had qualities we are inclined to associate with the gutter press. It was to the fore in exposing fraudulent promotion schemes and swindlers of every description, and carried on its own violent private feuds with public men. Its influence on Parliament and political changes was immense, and even Prime Ministers feared it.

It was the pioneer, too, in establishing the modern system of having correspondents stationed at capital cities and seats of war abroad and constantly beat its contemporaries in being first with the news. In 1870 its advertising revenue was of the order of £1,500 a day, and it was estimated that an issue consumed 70 tons of paper and 2 tons of ink. Nor was it the old-fashioned thing of 4 pages: its normal size was 24 pages, or 144 columns.

When it made mistakes it made them courageously. It warned the public of the misery and ruin which would attend what it called 'the railway mania' when trains were running at the unprecedented speed of 15 miles an hour and persisted in this attitude despite the fact that it resulted in the loss of £3,000 a week in railway advertising. And it was notable not only for paying the highest price for articles but by giving generous pensions to staff members who retired.

The attitude of *The Times* to Ireland and her troubles is another week's story. After disclosure of the Pigott forgery, Parnell sued the paper for £100,000 for libel, but settled for £5,000.

There's something fishy here

This week I should like to venture a little comment on a subject which has many aspects and is much talked and written about, sometimes praised, sometimes condemned as a gross public scandal, occasionally denounced as a ripe example of the stage the country has come to.

No, I don't mean hooliganism, the price of drink, dance halls, or even bingo. I mean navigation and fishing, and those two pursuits are much tied up with each other. I claim to know a bit about both, unlike most other people, who think they know EVERYTHING about them.

Ireland is a small island in which it is impossible to stand anywhere without being within 55 miles of the sea; and a glance at the map shows that, by reason of the profusion of great lakes and rivers, the country is internally waterlogged. Yet everywhere it is difficult – often impossible – to get fresh fish at a reasonable cost.

Poaching is rampant all over the country but any fish illegally taken (particularly the noble salmon) is intended exclusively for the black market. I find the situation is inexplicable, and made by no means the clearer by any babble from politicians, pisciculturists or those wisest of men, economists.

I am sure most readers will share a memory of my own very early youth. In those days one did not require a clear mind or a handy newspaper to know that a certain morning of the week was a Friday morning; lurid banshee shrieks from the street or road outside betokened that a woman was on her rounds with a basket selling fish, usually real fresh herrings, at possibly tuppence each. She is now as obsolete as men wearing wigs and swords.

Technical people say that our sea-going fishermen are lazy and incompetent and that the steam trawlers they use are quite unsuitable – far too small and unfitted for proper cruises of 8 or 9 days. Well, their predecessors used sail, which made their trips far more unpredictable as to distance and duration, and yet they landed immeasurably more fish. The poor folk of the West lived on fish and potatoes, and it is true that the currach is the most primitive of vessels.

If we are not to be forced to the conclusion it is the men who are different, we may fall back on the theory that the distribution system of the fish trade is ruinously inefficient. One hears of a big catch being landed in Donegal but having to be dumped in a fish-meal factory owing to the prohibitive cost of transporting the catch and marketing it in the cities and bigger towns. It is a comforting thought, even if the comfort is a bit perverse, but it does suggest that such chaos could be somehow remedied.

But another possibility, not lightly to be dismissed, is that Irish people as a whole do not like fish. Certainly where fish is to be had, the choice available to them is laughably limited: herring (perhaps), whiting and cod. Shellfish such as lobster or oyster is out of the question at the best of times owing to cost, and most people hold that mackerel is uneatable unless cooked within 12 hours of being landed. Plaice and sole are regarded as luxuries, sinful to buy.

I have personally done some sailing, mostly in Dublin Bay and thereabouts, and there is no more exhilarating way of passing the time if one has a good boat, the skill to sail it and a fair breeze. Mackerel hauled in from lines trailing at the stern taste indescribably wonderful if flung on the pan of a good primus stove almost before they are dead. But there are other fish, too.

What does the reader think of the following list? Sennit, Wall, Granny, Thief, Seizing, Diamond.

Would you fry, boil, stew or roast them? No, faith – for they are knots that are familiar to a good yachtsman, and you can't eat ropes (which we yachtsmen always call 'sheets').

177

To the good landlocked folk of Carlow I would say this: never take out a sailing boat alone unless you have experience and know how to handle it, even on quite inland water. For then you might find yourself not only IN THE CART but, far worse, IN THE BARROW!

Taking too much for granted

All of us every day make use of small items and services so constantly and casually that we usually become quite unaware of them. But if you happen to be walking across the Curragh of Kildare and, quite alone, decide to light a cigarette, the discovery that you haven't got a match can be a calamitous shock.

It can be an occurrence that seems to darken the sun. And if you found you had a box of matches all right but not a solitary cigarette, you would probably conclude that earlier in the day you had taken leave of your senses.

The fact is that we take too much for granted.

That was the sentiment which came into my head at the start of the bus strike several weeks ago, when I was living just outside Dublin city. True, the strike was countrywide but the importance of public transport in a big city is far more vital than anywhere in rural Ireland.

In effect it is the city's bloodstream, and the total absence of buses caused something not far from absolute paralysis. As in all big modern cities, very few people live in the inner warrens and hives of work; they live as far out as they can and daily commute to their offices, factories or shops.

And when the carrying firm is in fact a State monopoly, a strike is an absolute thing. It could in many cases impose severe hardship, sometimes perhaps death, though this is not the place to argue out the wrongs and the rights of the occurrence. It is however worth noting that initially the men struck in defiance of the advice of their union leaders.

The worthwhile question is this: how did the Dublin people manage for those five weeks?

I am delighted to report that they managed very well, often achieving miracles of improvisation, and the heroes who shone most brightly were the owners of private cars. To wait at a bus stop on a lonely suburban road was to be certain of a lift into town, and in a matter of minutes. Alas, the snag was getting a lift out again, for hanging about traffic-packed city streets gives no clue as to destination.

As is usual in most civil catastrophes, the situation had many diverting aspects. The eye was confronted with motor vehicles of unbelievable antiquity, bicycles which had probably not been on a public road since 1919, and a veritable swarm of scooters, tandems, motor-bikes and even bath chairs. There was no limit, provided the 'yoke' had wheels.

And there was, of course, always the horse, though I cannot imagine where one could park a horse. Finally, a great number of people were forced to acknowledge an astonishing conclusion: that is that they could still walk, and that this exercise did them no harm.

Not a few (call them eccentrics if you will) came to the conclusion that buses were a curse, devices to make the able-bodied into effete wastrels, and an insult to civilisation.

The British in wartime plugged the phrase IS YOUR JOURNEY REALLY NECESSARY? It was a shrewd and effective question, for in those years overladen transport was being choked by people whose business was mainly to wander about and gaze at shop windows.

That question was much asked in Dublin of late, and in thousands of cases the short honest answer was NO. But that meant disastrous business for cinemas and theatres.

What was done by the Government, itself largely responsible for the crisis? Next to nothing at all. A small number of dirty Army lorries (I was in two) were run between selected suburban points and the city centre. Each Minister has a Mercedes-Benz to go about in.

It is not right, I think, to be frivolous about an affair of this kind. A city is a monstrously artificial invention, and its inhabitants are pathetically vulnerable from every angle. My own form of personal solace was to meditate on what would happen if there was a countrywide strike of the staff of the Electricity Supply Board.

Think that one out. Tens of thousands of homes would have no heat or light. Many water and sewerage systems would collapse, since many have pumping installations. No telephone to call doctor or priest if you are suddenly very sick, and no prospects of the essential operation even if you do get to hospital.

I'll pile on a final horror: no Teiefis Eireann!

Do you like doing it yourself?

In a long, holy and brilliant life I have done many things but this week let me mention just one little sortie of mine. Several years ago I was directed, in two succeeding years, to go to London as 'observer' rather than as a member to the annual congress of the Royal Society for the Prevention of Accidents.

My interest was motor traffic and road safety but that did not dilute my astonishment at the unbelievable awkwardness of that body's title. The Society is still very much alive.

Its congress has to be seen to be believed. It is held in an enormous hall in the Westminster area and the delegates attending, nearly all representing some local authority, amounted to about 4,000. Not one of them was in the least bit shy in standing up and haranguing the multitude for five minutes, not infrequently on some irrelevant pet theme of his own. It was a startling spectacle of democracy in action.

Of course the Society takes cognisance of road accidents but I was moderately surprised to note that it did not permit this branch of disaster to be an obsession: far from it, indeed, for its records and experience showed that the great bulk of the accidents awaiting mankind lay elsewhere. And in the most surprising places.

Know where is the most dangerous place to be? At home! That is not a facetious sally like saying that since 90 per cent of the people die in their beds, being in bed is very dangerous. That being at home is danger – is a fact, statistically established beyond argument.

And the most accident-prone are the very young or those past middle age, with most of the accidents arising from the carelessness of people in the age-groups between.

By the hundred annually are measured the number of youngsters burnt to death from falling into unprotected open fires. A somewhat similar mortality arises from youngsters pulling down on top of themselves open saucepans of boiling water from the top of cookers or ranges.

The word 'accident' does not necessarily mean death, and thousands of domestic accidents merely leave the victim crippled or mutilated for life. Apart from the youngsters drowned in baths, a great number of others are severely scalded.

We all acknowledge the perils of the highway but it is fair enough to call the stairs a highway and, next to the kitchen, it is the most perilous part of an average small house. The young and the old are insecure of foot (the old often further endangered by failing sight) and the cases of people falling downstairs are nearly uncountable.

Even if one fall or several in the same house can be traced directly to a tear in the carpet or an ill-fitting stair-rod, the defect is hardly ever put right; this is probably on the same baseless principle that lightning cannot strike twice in the same place. Stairs have another hazard, and I confess I have personally had more than one painful encounter with it.

I mean falling upstairs; in this case it is your head which is bound to have the worst of things, and a fractured knee-cap is a commonplace.

A shockingly large number of deaths occur in the home due to electrocution, with a somewhat lower number in towns due to gas poisoning. Poisoning in many other forms abounds, such as sheer carelessness in mistaking a bottle of some lethal cleaning fluid for medicine the doctor ordered, or unthinkingly using some genuine foodstuff which has been so long in the house that it has become putrid. Nor are you safe in bed; hundreds are roasted annually through falling asleep with a cigarette alight, and occasionally the whole house becomes a flaming tomb for everybody in it.

I mentioned electrocution. Apart from defective appliances, this often arises from wiring being carried out by the man-of-the-house himself, either to save money or to show he knows as much about the subject as any damn electrician. And that pinpoints my main point – that homes are ever becoming more dangerous by reason of the modern Do It Yourself mania.

Nothing easier than to build a concrete wall in your garden, of course, but when a gust of wind blows it down on top of your little daughter, I suppose doubt begins to creep in.

Any man who is rational and has a decent pair of hands can himself instal a heavy chandelier in the living-room, but there is always a good chance that it will fall down and kill somebody. Which of us is not smart enough to make his own shoes, radio and even TV sets?

From advertisements I notice that this lunacy is taking a new direction. Several firms (but mostly Japanese) are offering such articles as bicycles, scooters and even small cars in the ordinary intact form cheaply, but far more cheaply in what they call Kit form.

The theory is that anybody but an imbecile can assemble such things himself – 'at home, in his spare time'. One American firm is offering a tiny aeroplane on this basis. Soon we'll all be assembling our own rockets, possibly with nuclear warheads.

It would be better for most of us to assemble our thoughts, and stop this dangerous fooling.

Moore of the Melodies

Strange thing that with all the opportunities offered by TV, no decent hack has given us a piece on Tom Moore. I will probably have to do it myself. Moore, man of intellect, superb at adulation, prince of leg pullers, had the strangest of careers.

For a quarter of a century he had £500 a year for writing words to supplied music. When Longman's thought they would like a long poem 'on an Eastern subject' they paid Moore 3,000 guineas in advance, and eventually he came up with *Lalla Rookh*. I too have had dealings with Longman's and can testify that their treatment of me was similarly generous.

The beauty of the old airs which form his 'Melodies' tends to mask the fact that his verse was shocking doggerel.

> *The minstrel boy to the wars has gone,*
> *In the ranks of death you'll find him.*
> *His father's sword he has girded on,*
> *And his wild harp slung behind him.*

All right. Let's look at that.

The scene is the austere office of the Commanding Officer.
The Minstrel Boy has been frogmarched in by two guards.

C.O.: Ah, Private Rafferty. I noticed you particularly on parade this morning. What is that damned weepan you have there?

M.B.: A sword, sor.

C.O.: How dare you call that weepan a sword! Where in hell did you get it?

M.B.: It's me father's, sor, yer honour.

C.O.: I should have you court-martialled for disgracing your uniform with such a weepan. Your father's? I suppose he used it at the battle of Clontarf?

M.B.: No sor. Th'oul fella lives at Booterstown, not Clontarf.

C.O.: Hand that weepan to the quarter-master, get a real one, and then do a term of fourteen days C.B. Dismiss!

C.O. (*as detachment reaches door*): Halt! About turn! Rafferty!

M.B.: Yessor.

C.O.: What's that damned thing on your back?

M.B.: My wild harp, sor.

C.O.: *Your what?*

M.B.: It's me wild harp slung behind me.

C.O.: Well it's the first time I ever heard of a harp as an item of combat equipment. Can you play it?

M.B.: Yes, sor. I can play 'Kitty of Coleraine' and 'The Lanty Girl.'

C.O.: Ah, an interest in the fair sex, Rafferty? How many strings are on it?

M.B.: Thirty five, sor.

C.O.: Very well. Hand that apparatus in to the quarter-master. In addition to fourteen days C.B. I sentence you to thirty five lashes. Dismiss!

The comers and goers

Let me set out one word which is new, mysterious, fully understood by nobody, very important, possibly disreputable, by many thought fraudulent and detestable and sometimes defined as the name of this country's second most important industry – TOURISM.

It is, as I have said, new, and the multiple façades of its meaning may be gleaned from the French word *tour*, which my dictionary says has the following meanings in English:

Turn, going round, winding; revolution; turn; circumference; circuit; trick; feat; order; manner; twist; strain; lathe; turning box; tour, trip; valance (of bed); turn (act); front, foretop (of hair) . . .

Now it is not good enough to say that tourism is just a fancy new name for 'taking holidays'. Obviously it is much more than that because it entails a populational upheaval, a considerable social mix-up and also financial transactions which in sum are formidable.

In this country most of us doubt the volume of the tourist trade as given annually by Bord Fáilte because many of the figures are estimates and anyway it is impossible to segregate in the total of visitors which are properly called tourists (or foreigners visiting this country) and which are Irish people, mostly from Britain, coming home for a few weeks to visit relatives. But given that the figures are roughly right, is it a desirable business?

One objection to it is that it is sharply seasonal. The off/on nature of the employment it affords in hotel and catering establishments must cause hardship and disruption to those who work in the business, and proprietors are pressed to carry out capital investment which will yield a very uncertain return when one considers the many imponderable and unpredictable factors which govern tourist traffic, from Irish weather to the varying industrial and financial conditions abroad.

One does not have to exaggerate the close and considerable ties which exist between this country and the USA (where there is usually no shortage of money) but it is a fact that, Shannon notwithstanding, the numbers of holiday-makers here from the US is disappointingly small; the majority of such people regard Paris as the ideal jumping-off point for an exploration of the Old World, and direct jet flights to that city are nearly as short and convenient as is the stop at Shannon.

Furthermore, the spread of tourist traffic here is very uneven, some places getting an absurdly large and undeserved share of the spoils.

No visitor to Ireland would dare be going away without having seen the lakes of Killarney, Galway Bay and maybe the Glens of Antrim, and also loafing around historic Dublin, but I would personally say that Wicklow, for its astonishing variety of mountain, strand, woodland and river, is the most attractive and beautiful country in Ireland, but little visited by foreigners.

I suppose in tourist traffic terms the word 'unspoilt' is one of praise but I doubt if publicans or hoteliers would agree: they would probably substitute 'neglected'.

These thoughts were provoked by a curious personal experience. When the present writer had the honour to be a very young fellow, his parents used to take a house for the months of July and August in Skerries. This is a pleasant little seaside town about 18 miles north of Dublin and has long been that city's resort for holidays of the 'family' kind as distinct from Bray, which is a shrill gaudy place full of noise, honky-tonks and neon.

I revisited Skerries on the 31st of last month to check on something and noted many changes, mostly for the worse, though strange to say several of the old thatched houses in the town survive.

It was my first sight of Red Island, which calls itself a holiday camp but which looked to me at least from the outside as the nearest thing imaginable to a Nazi extermination camp (but I don't mean that it is necessarily not a nice place to stay). It may be that the date of my visit was unfortunate but I must report that so far as visitors were concerned, the place was almost deserted and the few I did encounter all seemed to be English.

Here was apparently another aspect of tourism. In recent years it seems that all Irish people who can afford to take a real holiday away from home make sure to spend it anywhere except in Ireland, and for many years now a favourable exchange rate of currency has induced thousands of Irish people to go to Spain. And France, Germany and Italy have long had their own attractions for our people.

I personally know the Rhineland better than I know the valley of the Liffey or sweet vale of Avoca, but somehow I don't feel an unpatriotic renegade.

I'll finish with a true story about the late R.M. Smyllie, famed Editor of the *Irish Times*. He was on holiday in Germany at the outbreak of the 1914 war and was immediately arrested. He protested that he was an Irishman, not British, and demanded that he be sent back to Ireland.

'*Irland?*' the fat, puzzled sergeant said incredulously. He took down an enormous atlas in the police station, laboriously turned over the pages and finally slammed it shut.

'*Existiert nicht!*' he roared, and Smyllie was locked up for the duration.

Time for the holliers again!

Readers will remember that I recently wrote some notes here on TOURISM, questioning certain aspects of this industry, particularly the results of its essentially seasonal nature and the distortion and disequilibrium arising from the marked unevenness of its impact on Ireland, both territorially and as to people.

Certain highly publicised spots get the bulk of the trade and the money while other places, just as admirable, get next to nothing. Well, there seems no easy answer to such problems – except, perhaps, to tell foreign visitors on arrival that they will damn well go wherever the big buses bring them! What an opportunity for lone Mountmellick!

Today I would like to attempt some remarks on a subject cognate to tourism, namely, an ordinary Irishman's attitude to taking his annual summer holidays. I will set the matter out in the form of a dialogue between two old pals who casually meet.

'Ah, Tom, the bould man. Right well you're looking.'

'And why shouldn't I? You're not looking too bad yersalf aither.'

'Any holidays yet?'

'The what was that?'

'Holidays. Did you take any yet?'

'Course I did. Three weeks, and I never enjoyed meself so much. Made a new man of me.'

'Where did you go? I mean, was it Madrid or just Lahinch?'

'Are you sarious?'

'I'm always sarious. If it was Vienna, can't you just say so? Or is it a top secret?'

'Listen here. If you want to suggest I'm some sort of a mad willy-the-wisp at my time of life, I suppose I'll have to pretend to laugh at your poor idea of a joke. For yer information, I didn't traipse across to Moscow aither. No sir!'

'Well where did you spend yer holidays?'

'I spent them at home like a dacent man, where I'm properly fed, don't have to sleep in a damp bed and put up with the bad indescribable language of Frenchies or Japanees. Nor Cockney bowsies naither.'

'Well holy mackerel! You didn't go away at all?'

'Indeed and I did – and every day. A day-trip to Portmarnock wan day, maybe to Maynooth the next. And I took care to have a good lie-up in the mornings, too.'

'Me dear man, did you never hear of the great benefits of a change of scene, a change of air and meeting complete strangers? You must be the only character alive today who never heard of the great benefits of a complete break. That has been acknowledged for centuries, man. The important thing is change.'

'Is that so? *Change?* I prefer to keep me change in me own pocket.'

'Living away is nearly as cheap as living at home.'

'You talk of the benefits of a complete break, acknowledged for centuries. Is that so? What centuries? The idea of holidays at all, of any kind, is quite recent. In the day of Charles Dickens the way to clean a filthy chimney was to send a young boy up it. Slavery! Come across to this pub and I'll stand you a pint. I've still a few bob of my holidays money left.

'Tell you another thing – and stop slopping that pint about! As you probably know, I'm on a diet. Even in a decent hotel (if I could afford it) I would be regarded as a nuisance.'

'Or a pest.'

'And furthermore, if I could persuade them to attend to me special diet, I'll go bail there would be an extra charge. Once you don't fit into their plan for the mass-production of their dirty grub, you're a special case. If yer stomach isn't right, you'll pay through the nose for it. And if you complain, out you go!'

'Of course a good boarding house might look after you OK?'

'And be ett alive be fleas in the middle of the night?'

'Ah now I don't know.'

'Tell me this. What about yerself? Have you taken any holliers yet?'

'No. I start in about eight days from now.'

'And where are you going?'

'Aw, Skerries for a fortnight. Go there every year with the wife and kids.'

'*Skerries?*'

'Yiss. You see, there's bags of sand down there. The very man for the kids.'

'I'll say no more. Next year I might change me own ideas and take a trip to Constanty Nopel.'

Spending has problems

An Irish firm recently offered a prize of £300 'to be spent in 24 hours'. I did not examine this strange offer very closely as, to be eligible, one had to buy a refrigerator.

Frankly, I don't need a refrigerator and cannot help regarding things that are kept in them with suspicion. I may mention in passing that there is something far more terrible than the commonplace fridge: it is called the Deep Freeze.

I came into collision with the Deep Freeze last Christmas when an old friend whom I accidentally met in Dublin town invited me into an expensive restaurant 'for a bite'. I was bitten all right. He suggested some salmon, and I thoughtlessly agreed to this.

Only after several weeks' appalling illness did I realise that it had come from the Deep Freeze and had possibly been caught in 1946. Archaeological treasures are fine, but not on the plate between your knife and fork.

But this £300 to be spent in 24 hours? Let us suppose that the condition is exactly that, that the sum of £300, no more and no less, must be got rid of in that short space of time. I think it would be a most difficult thing to do – it might even be impossible. You could not, for instance, buy something worth considerably more than £300, adding your own money to make up the difference. Anything worth less than £300 would also be a rupture of the bargain.

Can you think of any surefire way of getting rid of this sum by buying something?

Let's see (and discard) some of the obvious ideas.

Walk into a bookie's shop and put it all on a horse? No. That sounds simple but would fail, for any bookie in his senses would refuse the bet. Just try putting on a fiver and you'll know what I mean. Irish bookmakers regard bets as money into the kitty. They don't see anything funny about bets on horses which romp home. They suspect a 'job' has been pulled and pay only with enormous reluctance. The punter feels slightly ashamed of himself while he pockets the greasy reward of his courage.

The words 'buy' or 'spend' must be given their full, simple value. When you buy something, you must get it right away and have the use of it. This rules out a great variety of purchases. It is unlikely but still possible that a highly undesirable tumbledown cottage would be on the market: but you couldn't buy it.

No matter how courteous and gallant the owner, the lawyers would have to set about putting the deeds in order, meanwhile holding your cash or cheque strictly in suspense. This foostering would take at least a fortnight, and your 24-hour transaction would simply not exist.

Well, how about buying a car? Out of the question. No doubt a good second-hand car could be got for £300 but the day has not dawned when you could buy such a machine and drive in it. Very likely it would have to be taxed but even if it is taxed, it would be illegal for you to put it on the road without insurance. And that would take a week.

The same can be said of almost anything that is designated Property. Lawyers, busybodies and inter-ferers are involved, with inevitable delay. If you went into a highclass outfitter's, sent for the manager and told him you wanted to spend £300 – no more, no less – on clothing for yourself, he would probably smile affably, discuss the whole mystique of dress since earliest times and keep you engaged in conversation until the police had arrived.

The same would be true of attempts to buy wallpaper, raspberries for making 7,000 lb of jam, ornamental Chinese lacquerwork, 6,000 sq. yards of trelliswork to secure privacy in your garden, or even 800 blankets to keep you warm. It's not sufficient to want something and readily produce the money to pay for it.

It must be a REASONABLE something. Try buying £300 worth of invisible ink and you will almost certainly find yourself in some dungeon where spies are stored. Even outsize expenditure on photographic materials would be dangerous for the same reason.

Is there then anything left? Well, a fur coat is a possibility but you would have to be a woman and be sure you knew rabbit from mink. Even then some hugger-mugger entailing delay might be involved, for the better stores probably keep their top class coats in a secret store in some remote village such as Mulhuddart. In any case I've never heard of a fur coat worth exactly £300.

Could you perhaps buy a whole collection of things in total worth £300? Without hesitation I would say NO. It is all very well to lay out tenpence on a quarter pound of Marie biscuits, 3d on a bar of chocolate and one and eightpence on postage stamps.

Perfecting such transactions takes time, and that 24 hours can be a viciously narrow term. Even if it wasn't you would lose count.

In a last desperate plunge, when in a state of collapse from fatigue and worry, you would probably buy a radiogram, bringing your grand total to £315, with the taxi to pay on top of that.

My own choice in a situation of this kind is automatic. Give me, I say, what I am well used to by now and am no longer terribly afraid of. I mean poverty.

The night that I nearly died

Here you are – Hilaire Belloc wrote many years ago – twenty-one years of age and you've never written a dictionary. Yes, I suppose that shows a certain laziness, a want of enterprise. But let me myself make a comparable but perhaps more serious complaint. Here you are, I say, now around 50 years of age and you've never had a heart attack!

Does such a situation call for . . . shame? The reader must decide that question for himself but most doctors find that a heart attack is not the result of organic disease or an actual cardiac lesion but due to physical stress – to the heart-owner making unreasonable and sustained demands on his most precious of physical machines. Such a person is usually far more fastidious as to the care of his stomach, which is really a crude sort of a bag and fairly well able to put up with abuse; and even when it does go on strike, its owner may not feel very well but at least his life is not in danger. The heart is a different and much more delicate matter.

Needless to say, I am not raising this issue from the academic or literary standpoint. It is prompted by an alarming experience of my own dating back to a few weeks ago, and I might be doing somebody a service by giving some brief account of it here.

One night, feeling a bit tired, I decided to go to bed early and by ten p.m. was snugly ensconced in my luxurious pallet with that most cheerful of sleeping inducements, i.e. a good book. I was alone in the house but felt restful and at peace. Just what happened next it is not easy to say. I think I was leaning outwards to extinguish a cigarette in a bedside ashtray. Apparently in the middle of doing so I passed out and fell bodily out of bed on to the floor on my face. When my be-na-tee came home later, she found me thus unconscious in a heap, the region of my right eye and ear now turning black from the contusion of the fall.

Frantic telephone calls to a number of local doctors brought no result, though the time was perhaps 11.30 p.m. and not really late. Eventually a man was contacted comparatively far away and he came promptly.

'A massive coronary, I'm afraid,' he said, after a brief examination. 'We must get an ambulance at once.'

This was done and, attired in pyjamas and dressing gown, I came bleakly back to life in a hospital a considerable distance outside Dublin. Curiously, the doctor I found confronting me wore no white coat and no stethoscope protruded from any pocket. Also, I found it hard to understand what he was saying. But as my mind gradually sharpened, the truth dawned on me. He was a priest and he was administering the last rites.

Dear reader, it can be a scaring experience.

When the doctors, three of them at least, got to work, they were not long in coming to the common conclusion that I had, in fact, had no heart attack, coronary or otherwise. What then had happened? Well, first, there had been some sort of kidney failure or infection. This in turn led to contamination of the blood, and the sudden pass-out exploit was due to the supply of the wrong sort of blood to the brain.

After some days I managed to arrange a transfer to a better-organised and more convenient hospital, and it is from there I send these notes. I now feel fine but the doctor says that, after innumerable tests of it, there is an alien substance in my blood-stream. The immediate problem is to find out what is causing it. And I have been given to understand that such a problem is no push-over joke. And if I leave hospital without knowing the remedy, I am liable to another similar collapse. I seem to be in a mess that is not a little bit ridiculous.

It is commonly agreed that the man who talks about his illness (or more usually his operation) is a fearful bore. Well, I honestly claim that what I have written here is useful. Why is that? It happens that I am a member of The Voluntary Health Insurance Board, whose address is 9 South Leinster Street, Dublin 2. The Board will send any applicant a brochure explaining its activities but they may be very briefly summarised as follows: a client may buy annually, according to his means and needs, a varying number of units covering (a) accommodation in hospital, and (b) medical attendance; no benefit is payable unless in respect of expenses incurred within a hospital.

I will conclude by saying, testily, that any decent, ordinary person who is not a member of this organisation is an improvident fool!

Getting well is
plenty of trouble

My disclosure last week on The Night That I Nearly Died (absolutely genuine) brought no telegrams of sympathy and encouragement and I did not notice any flowers or wreaths arriving on the offchance of a funeral. Of course my report was preliminary and incomplete and I must now be careful to avoid becoming the classic nuisance who bores everybody he meets to tears with a long detailed story of his operation (in my case, operations).

Yet one, em . . . incident I absolutely insist on recounting, giving my reason for doing so afterwards. Ever hear the word *biopsy*? In meaning it could be said to be the opposite of autopsy, which is the examination of specimens from the body after death. With a biopsy you want for examination a bit of a man's body while he is still alive, in my case a specimen of my kidney tissue.

How is this got? Easy, man. The surgeon drives a thing (which I haven't seen) known in the trade as a 'needle' into the patient's back, far in until it reaches and penetrates his kidney. That the word 'needle' is misleading is plain enough when I reveal that it is hollow so that it can extract a specimen of the kidney tissue and so, if plain language be sought, it should not be a needle but a neat dagger.

A local anaesthetic is used for this job. I felt the little prick betokening the entry of the anaesthetic fluid but almost immediately, before that fluid had time to act, I felt the 'needle' being rammed in through my sensitive, noble flesh. Inward and onward, and boys-a-dear, I can certify that no word in print could describe what I went through or, indeed, what went through me. I was flabbergasted to be told afterwards when back in bed in a state of collapse that the mastermind of a surgeon had in fact 'missed the kidney'. My miraculous feat of endurance had all been for nothing.

And what is my reason for revealing that extraordin-ary occurrence here? Just to ask why it should be allowed to happen in a closed and private operating room rather than (in the best traditions of cine-variety) on the stage of the Ritz, Carlow. Surely some magician has already sawn a woman in half there?

Well, I quickly left that hospital and went home before I heard somebody say, 'Ah well, we'll have another try.' How am I now? I feel quite well, can eat my dinner like a man, but clinically I might be still at death's door. Somehow, I feel there is an obligation on me to DO SOMETHING, though I'm not certain what. I have been ill. Very well. Is it not the obvious thing to reconcile myself to a period of convalescence, like Mr Harold Macmillan? But that is easier said than done. I cannot remember ever having been convalescent before, and I find the very word awkward to spell.

I know that nowadays it does not mean a bath-chair, a nurse, a diet of beef tea and gruel. (That would just make me sick.) No, our modern idea is brighter, bigger, more courageous. Even that 'long sea voyage' of Queen Victoria's day is out of favour but how about a recuperative trip to the United States?

Well, here we have to pause. As I write two distinguished Irishmen have recently returned from the United States – the Editor of this newspaper, and our Taoiseach, Mr Sean Lemass. I think a lot depends on the capacity in which you go to the States, perhaps more on the capacity in which you are received.

To judge from his despatches home, our Editor refused to be harried and probably was never in a helicopter in his life, no more than I was. He was looking around with astute observation and talking only to the people who interested him. But Lemass, if the radio accounts can be trusted, was being boiled, stewed, grilled, roasted and filleted for about 18 hours a day, compelled to make a great number of solemn speeches and eat countless dinners.

He was getting a treatment stepped up in intensity to twice what President Kennedy got in this country – and two days and nights of that sort of thing would KILL myself. Nothing would entice me to visit the States.

But where else is there to go – where else is there that is safe? Killarney is always there, by kind permission of the Germans, but it is always raining there. All the seaside resorts are locked up and gloomy at this time of the year. Even a winter trip to London would entail the risk of getting mixed up in some awful scandal. And the south of France is out because I can't speak the sort of French the people there can understand, and anyway I can't play cards.

The last resort (no pun!) seems to be Dublin: get digs there for ten days or so and make day trips to great centres of art and enterprise such as Guinness's Brewery, the Galleries, the Library, the Museum, the Esso Petroleum works, the Gasometer and . . . well . . . the most famous of the hospitals.

At one of them I might even be privileged (provided I looked sufficiently like a rubber-necking American) to be a witness at a biopsy operation. Heavens, what strange bliss that would be!

Risks we take on
Sunday morning

A peculiarity of the Catholic religion is that Sunday morning congregations show a reluctance to disperse. Could it be a weakness for prying into other people's prosperity or the lack of it as exhibited in their Sunday morning exhibition of themselves in their best attempt at dress? Or could it be a thirst for scandalous gossip?

A forlorn curiosity about what was the outcome of that coursing match held the previous day ten miles away? No, I think this tendency to dawdle is innocent, a sort of genial weekly pause on life's journey, an opportunity to ask some fellow-dawdler how his wife is keeping. (Yes, that's the phrase – as if his wife was some sort of a mummy, kept presentable by preservatives but liable to go bad at any moment!)

Yet, innocent though the pause be, it can be dangerous or – to use a rather milder word – alarming. It happened myself a few Sundays ago, and I cannot do better than set down in terse language what exactly happened, with no flourishes or hyperbole. The dead honest truth can be more terrifying than anything connected with Sweeney Todd, the Demon Barber of Fleet Street.

I was just standing there, looking around me. For the moment I hadn't a care in the world, though a very dirty letter from the income tax people had arrived the day before. What is Sunday morning for anyway, if not for delusions of immunity, peace, happiness ever after? Isn't a man entitled to his Sunday morning?

Another character of my own type approached. I knew him well and saw him every Sunday. He remarked that it was a lovely morning, thank God, and asked was I going to Croke Park. I told him I wasn't, that I thought people who had an interest in games should play them, not just gawk and then write angry letters to the papers. Anywhere else that uncouth answer would have started an argument – but not on Sunday morning. It seems the wrong time for profitless snarling. What was the use? Some other place, perhaps, with a few pints to encourage rhetoric, some other occasion.

On this particular morning we found a large man in an expensive belted coat bearing down on us. I knew him slightly and had long put him into the mental bracket labelled TYCOON. He had a pleasant way with him. He produced cigarettes and said it was a pleasant morning and how about a drive cross-country to get a breath of fresh air. Neither myself nor my friend saw anything wrong with this. Why not indeed? Both of us knew he had a large powerful car. After a bit of a walk we found it and got in.

Let me tell this little story as it gradually stole upon us. As we got into the country, our driver-host asked us how we thought the country was making out. I personally answered that I did not pretend to know, but that I seemed to be getting bills oftener. Though a perfect gentleman, the driver seemed to be a bit unnecessarily ferocious in his conversation. Did we know what a gallon of petrol cost?

We had to say no. Did we know the duty on tobacco? We didn't. I can only say that this tour, which seemed aimless, was an occasion of non-stop indignation, with the driver's speed increasing in direct ratio to his temper.

But he slowed down to a placid 20 m.p.h. or so to ask us in a steely voice what we thought the tour of Taoiseach Lemass in the United States had cost, and how many people were with him. We, ignorant of the price of petrol, did not know that either, but I was foolish enough to add that I thought it would be paid for by the State. The needle showed we were now doing 86 m.p.h. and about to enter Wicklow town.

I said I would very much like a cup of coffee and did in fact induce the host to pull up at a quiet hotel. He did in fact order a cup of coffee for me, a bottle of stout for my friend, and whispered the name of his own medicament into the ear of the waitress.

Slightly later he fired a piece of paper on the table, inviting us to have a look at that! It was a demand for £65 from the Dublin Corporation for rates on his private house.

'We are roasted first by the Leinster House crowd,' he roared, 'without any regard to the fact that we are due for another roasting by your men at City Hall.'

This remark showed myself up in the queerest attitude I could ever have adopted. I scarcely believed it was myself talking. I defended the rating authority. Central taxation, I said, was a severe but nebulous impost. You didn't know what you were getting in return. Sending troops to the Congo – I supposed that was fair enough but it was a remote thing.

But rates? You could see and feel the results. You had roads, footpaths, sewers, a water supply, public lighting, poor relief, mental hospitals, street signs – even a system of warning against hydrogen bombs. I excelled myself almost to the point of making it uncertain whether I was right for a lift home.

I do think that we should be at least polite to the rate collector. After all, he does not strike the rate, and we should not provoke him to strike us!

Hospitals offer poor fare

If a man repeats himself, you are inclined to say he is repetitious. That is, if you are a mild-mannered and easy-going person. But you are more likely to say something worse than that.

But the law of charity should prevail, for there may be a good excuse for saying the same thing a second time. For example, if nothing happened after you said to a barman, 'Give me a glass of whiskey,' you would be justified in repeating yourself. I have nothing so trivial in question here today. I feel my theme touches on the supernatural, for the occurrence seems to be outside the ordinary sequence of human affairs, far beyond anything that may be expected, extraordinary to the point of being frightening apart from being physically very painful.

Readers will remember my recent articles wherein I told of a sudden illness, my journey to hospital, and my slow recovery there. It's not a polite subject for literature – one's ills, tribulations and crises. Most people don't want to hear anything about them, having enough troubles of their own to get foostered about and being anxious to do nothing but mind their own business.

That's fair enough, but there might be a wider public interest involved in what I have to say – the question of hoodoo, a mysterious personal curse, black magic or the secret incantations of witch-doctors. Just because we in Ireland don't live in the jungle is not to say we are free from occult and evil forces. I do not want to dismay or alarm anybody, but strange forces may be at work among us, and to be warned is to be fore-armed. Let me tell of what happened last Saturday.

I was in good form, bright and cheerful, and made a slight trip to buy papers and also some of those pernicious things called cigarettes. To a large extent, all was right with the world. My humble purchases completed, I took a bus home, and indeed arrived at the bus-stop which was my destination. It was then Force Sinister took over.

I can't describe in immediate detail what happened. In a way, it was pleasant. A nice rosy glow seemed to come over me. I wasn't in the least bit worried or upset. I felt things were being looked after – were in good hands. Indeed, I felt sort of happy.

But gradually, the image and the feeling changed. I found I was more uncertain of myself. I was in bed, but obviously not my own bed. Two men were doing something to my right leg and, unless I was mistaken, that new sensation I felt was extreme pain.

Well, time passed and, gradually, the story was pieced together. In getting off the bus, I had stepped on a stone or something of the kind, broken my leg at the ankle, fallen, and fainted away. I will probably never know what happened directly after that. Probably some passer-by raised the alarm and rang up for an ambulance.

The ambulance men brought me unconscious to a hospital not far away, where I was X-rayed. It was when two doctors were putting a temporary bandage (not plaster) on my leg that the light of sweet reason returned. I broke the same leg, almost at the same place, fifteen years ago, and I knew what I was in for: an initial period of extreme pain followed by a time – the length of which nobody could foretell – of complete immobilisation in a plaster cast. There is an immense difference in the time different people take for broken bones to 'knit'; on the previous occasion I had been 9 months out of action.

It is a woeful and dismal prospect, and I feel that ill-luck is not quite strong enough a term to denote this repetition of a major reverse in health. I feel I have done nothing to deserve it.

Initially, at least, it means life in hospital. No matter

how considerate and kind the nurses, this is no joke. The awful bang-bang starts at six in the morning, perhaps only an hour after the patient has managed to lapse into an uneasy sleep. Hours of turmoil follow, with fuss about washing and shaving and even saying prayers. For those in extreme pain it can be very trying. In fact it can be brutal.

There is one last thing which must be said, not about any particular hospital, but about them all: the food is terrible. Not personal experience alone justifies this dictum; many, many other people have been forced to the same conclusion.

The general feeling is that while hospital staffs big and small have given minute study to medicine, surgery and nursing generally, they have given hardly any attention to the extremely technical science of mass catering. No restaurant which dispensed 'hospital food' would last a week.

There is another source of intense suffering in hospital, even in a very small ward. I mean the other fiendish patient who has brought a radio in with him and insists on having this thing blazing loudly all day no matter what the condition of his fellow patients. The extraordinary thing is that hospital authorities do nothing to stop or restrain this horrible practice. In the modern hospital, of course, each bed is connected to a central radio installation, and each patient provided with headphones if he requires them.

I cannot forget what one man told me he saw happening to a fellow-patient; this unfortunate man was anointed to the lilt of 'The Blue Danube' and later died to strains of 'Smoke Gets In Your Eyes'.

I hope most of my own convalescence – if we call it that – will be spent at home. Radio there is completely under control, unlike myself in the use of my legs.

Mind your language!

Just imagine this situation: it is raining in torrents and on the road there is a man with a car. The car is stopped but the man has the hood up. WOULD YOU PITY HIM?

Not so simple, that question. The answer depends on the country – nay, the hemisphere – in which the scene is laid. If the man with the car is in the United States, then he is in a mess, for there the word hood means what we call bonnet, and obviously his engine is banjaxed. In passing, let me record my own sense of nostalgia at mention of a car's hood.

It seems to evoke the ghost of the Model T and that fearsome thing presented by other makers in the early days – the One-Man Hood. The name suggested clearly that you could put the thing up yourself quite unaided, even on a lonely country road in a rainstorm. What it did not say was that you were expected to have the personal qualities of Henry Ford himself, the great funambulist Blondin, Jack Dempsey and Houdini.

I say it seriously when I express conviction that many an owner-driver (another obsolete term) met a lonely and terrible death in the thrall of a One-Man Hood. Compared with it, single-combat with an octopus was kid's stuff. Suppose, for argument's sake, you did get the thing up. How then could you be expected to drive the car home with two broken arms and a strained spine?

That was one of the menaces our fathers faced. Could there be any connection between the word hood and hoodlum?

This subject of divergency as between the English and the American languages was touched on last week by colleague Jack Juvenal. It is an interesting theme, and one that has been studied quite a bit by inquirers at the scientific level. Let us therefore have a glance.

At the time of the first verified white migration to America, it was a departure to the other side of the world.

The English language which emigrants from this part of the world brought with them became petrified, and many words and phrases still commonly in use in the States, by us regarded as American – even Hollywood – slang, were genuine English in use in Shakespeare's day. Such was, for instance, the phrase 'I guess', and genuinely ancient are such words as flap-jack, jeans, cesspool, greenhorn, bay-window, stock (meaning cattle) and fall (in the sense of autumn).

But the subject is complicated because the immigration of English speakers from Britain was followed by other immigrations from France, Germany and Holland, and all those people brought their linguistic furniture with them. But everybody freshly arriving in the New World was confronted with plants and animals that he had never heard of and was forced to adopt rough versions of Indian words: whence we have opossum, raccoon, woodchuck, moccasin and even tapioca.

But perhaps the most important factor in this situation of lingual flux was the fact that the English language is uniquely analytic (as distinct from being inflected like many European tongues – indeed, it has little more than the pathetic remnant of who, whom and whose) and it is infinitely versatile and twistable. Any foreigner can master what is called pidgin English in a few weeks, and to a large extent every man is entitled to make his own English.

In addition to that, the modern America is infinitely resourceful and even witty in inventing new words. We, pompously running to Greek, talk of the cinema but the Yank, far more adequately, talks of the movies. We have no equivalent of such words as dawnburster, rubberneck, bootlegger, triggerman, convertible and sedan (cars), fall-guy, lame-duck, hoopla, showbiz, tammany, or even shaymus (meaning an Irishman).

Even in serious, objective writing, Americans make very little distinction between slang and respectable improvisation in language. 'A.B.,' you may read in a State document, 'seemed a good guy but he was yellow.' At least nobody is in any doubt about the meaning of that. And there really isn't much difference between a trolley and a tram, or a lift and an elevator.

I feel printers and also careless writers have a lot to do with the formation of language. In Dublin there is a well-known amateur boxer who, though I believe of Irish birth, has a German name. I cannot say for certain what that name is, or what to call him in conversation. In countless newspaper articles he has been called (within the same article) Tiedt and Teidt.

I know enough German to be sure that IE has the sound of EE in the English 'seed' and that EI has the sound of the English word EYE. Therefore our boxer is either Mr TITE or Mr TEET.

But where does it end? For weeks in this very newspaper Richard Lea has been calling certain cows FRIESIANS. In fact they are FREISIANS, and on this occasion we can forget the pronunciation.

Upbringing, uplift, uproar

As I write these lines the morning paper records that on the previous day in the Dáil a Government deputy had complained that Mr Dillon had called Government backbenchers 'gutties'. In return he said that deputies in the opposite side of the House were nothing only a lot of 'plucked roosters'.

If any of the rest of us had a choice, I think most would elect to be a gutty, however much the term lacks precision. He may be badly dressed, loud and sometimes profane of language, but you no longer find him standing miserably at street corners. Indeed, the cornerboy is now largely obsolete as a social type.

The gutty is usually found indoors, sheltering behind a pint, and even looking sourly at television. A plucked rooster does not seem to have anything better to look forward to than the oven.

The question is, however – should dialogue of that kind take place in the Dáil at all? It is a deliberative assembly, concerned with the quiet and orderly presentation of views on important public issues, arrived at by members after objective cogitation, assisted perhaps by research in the library. The Standing Orders which guide the Chair make no allowances for interruptions, bellowed shouting, sneers, challenges or showers of personal abuse.

Needless to say, fisticuffs or gunplay (not unknown in similar other assemblies abroad) is absolutely out of order. Sometimes but not too often a Dáil deputy is 'named' for disorderly conduct, which means that there and then he has to leave the Chamber.

For all we know he may say to himself, 'Aw to hell with it, I'll go down to the bar and have a drink and maybe I can contact a few of the lads and get a game of poker going in a committee room.'

Noble rhetoric of the kind used by Burke and Grattan has fallen into completed disuse, very likely because Dáil deputies are quite incapable of it, and the only man who attempts old-style oratory, with variations of pitch and a wealth of florid gesture, is James Dillon, who can be a fascinating and impressive speaker and get punches home without appearing to be dealing in dirt at all.

But debates on the 212 per cent turnover tax were occasions of terrible scolding and scalding, with abuse and insults hurled readily across the floor with the greatest of freedom and violence. What are we to think of this? Must we conclude that many of the deputies are genuine gutties in upbringing, and that they are in their natural element in rows blistering with recrimination and threats?

The daily papers give such scenes great prominence and 'play' because readers demand a verbatim account of anything resembling a 'heave' or 'barney' at Leinster House. Usually however the report is accompanied by an austere editorial paternally reproving the main performers and denouncing such goings-on as 'disedify-ing', sometimes even 'disgraceful'. They deplore affronts to the dignity of parliament and moan of lapses in ordinary manners. Is that a parade of hypocrisy?

It is certainly not a realistic attitude in the world of today, when proceedings in any parliament minutely affect the lives of everybody. Deputies who betray bad temper at least give evidence that they understand what is under discussion and have strong feelings on the subject.

Their manner of speaking their minds may sometimes be unfortunate but surely lively debate is better than droning monologues and the featureless drool one has come to associate with the House of Lords at West-minster?

And is it reasonable to expect polish, reticence and delicate debating punctilio from a House that is largely composed of farmers, not a few of whom have handled the gun as well as the plough? Hardly. That is Ireland.

What one should rightly deplore in those 'exchanges' is the almost total lack of wit. If you call me a gouger, I'll call you a bowsie – but where does that get either of us? Too much of that sort of wordplay and both of us will come to be regarded by those present as bores who carry on our shoulders completely empty heads, people quite unfitted to be deputies. The fact is, of course, that prospective deputies are picked out at election times for their personal popularity in their home districts, for a known attitude of helpfulness, or indeed a man could command wide admiration for his skill with a fishing rod, or putting a horse at a fence.

The last quality considered is his potential as a parliamentarian, and in fact his ability to expertly judge public issues need not be called in question at all; under the party system he is just a vote, and undertakes to do as he is told.

A curiosity about Leinster House is the public gallery. It is cut off from the Chamber below by a screen of fine-mesh steel netting, no doubt giving some visitors the impression that they are beholding and hearing a den of wild animals. But such impression may be mutual, the deputies feeling that they are reasonably protected from those dangerous, unpredictable beasts, the People of Ireland.

It is painful to hear the Dáil now and again denounced as a 'talking-shop'. That is exactly what the word PARLIAMENT means.

Talking turkey

Christmas Day can have its little tragedies, too, and this year I was myself at the receiving end of what seems to be a massive threat to us all on a grand scale – the production and distribution of non-food. For many years an old friend has been sending me a turkey as a Christmas present. The turkey arrived this year as usual but hey! – it was in a special sort of a box! My ben-a-tee raised the alarm, said it was frozen, and that she had no idea of handling such matters. Nor had I. But the best that could be done was done, and the centre-piece of the Christmas dinner to which we all sat down was a generous portion of old bicycle tyres. I suppose I should not write with such precision, since I've never actually tried to eat old bicycle, but that turkey tasted as old bicycle tyres should. All the parsley sauce and salt in the world made no difference. It was awful.

Three things are possible. One – unlikely – is that the bird was a normal one from an Irish farm which had been killed early in December and frozen to guard against delays in marketing. A second possibility is that it was a 'battery' bird, artificially incubated, never released from the hatchery, fattened on synthetic food and chemicals, then killed and frozen. The third possibility was that it was a turkey from the real deep freeze which means that it could be a warrior who perished as long ago as 1958.

One way or another, the supplier was guilty of plain fraud. What he supplied and was paid for was not a turkey as people understand the word.

Yet the shock of this most unfestive encounter perhaps shows that I am as innocent as a child behind it all. In newspaper reports about the turkey market in London I had read references to 'mass-produced' and 'oven-ready'. I take that last term to mean what most of us understand by the word turkey, and that the other two are spook-turkeys full of chemicals and carrying bogus meat, possibly poisonous.

I did not think that this could happen in Ireland in the case of Christmas turkeys but this business, ghastly and probably dangerous to health as well, has been going on for at least a year in Dublin and the larger towns in the case of chickens, usually dubbed 'broiler chickens'. These are on view all the year round in the shops of grocers, butchers, fish-merchants and pub-licans, priced 7/6 and 12/-, ready to take away and pop in the oven (if raw) or put straight on the table for a cold banquet if already done to an enchanting brown. In some of the more opulent pubs, indeed, there is a spectacular revolving spit on which a chicken is being grilled as you watch.

I am told that the entire production procedure is automatic and that chickens of the desired weight are turned out by the 1,000 merely by controlling certain switches, dials and gauges after the machine has been charged with eggs, 'food' and certain varieties of 'nourishing rays'. The chicks when they emerge see neither mother nor daylight, ingest chemical nourish-ment and bogus fattening substances and are ready for slaughter – also mechanised – IN THREE WEEKS! To try to eat a chicken which has never seen a blade of grass or chased a worm is quite an experience but not one that any sensible person is likely to attempt twice.

Can this atrocious debauchment of nature also be undertaken with cattle? Could a calf be artificially suckled, reared and fattened in a magic manger or electronic stall to provide, ultimately, uneatable labora-tory beef?

And pigs? Can those brutes be managed, by means of a diabolical machine, so that by pressing a button an endless string of unearthly sausages come pouring out of the end of the humming installation?

I will not press this line of thought by inquiring whether human beings could be looked after this way also but I say it is amazing and shameful that public health authorities, central and local, have so far taken no notice of a money-making activity which may well be a threat to the well-being and even the lives of the people.

Many stupid, ignorant and unnecessary things are said in the Dáil. How about our hard-working deputies giving their attention to this sort of menace?

Enough is too much

Little Indian, Sioux or Crow,
Little frosty Eskimo,
Little Turk or Japanese –
O don't you wish you were like me!
You have curious things to eat,
I am fed on proper meat –
You must dwell beyond the foam,
But I am safe and live at home.

That was a neat, satirical way to express the outlook of . . . whom? The average Englishman? Or all of us? Unlikely as it may seem, the lines were written by Robert Louis Stevenson, whose personal infirmity ensured that he at least did not stay at home, damp and cold, but made him pack up and sail for sunny Samoa.

It is quite true that most of us shrink from the unaccustomed, whether it be in food, drink, weather, clothes or even music. With Dr Samuel Smiles (what an awful name!) our motto is TO STAY AT HOME IS BEST. But even at home there can be danger.

Look what happened to a lot of people recently. On their own dinner tables on Dec. 25 there was a wonderful succulent turkey and, with everything that went with it, it was immensely enjoyed. There was cold turkey the next day, of course, and that was quite acceptable. The evening after, one went to visit some friends, and they insisted on a bit of supper before parting. Well, yes, the cold turkey was all right. When one gets home, there is excitement in the house. A big turkey, a present from an old friend which had been held up in the post, had arrived. It meant, of course, hot roast turkey the next day, and the possibility of cold turkey for at least two days more. Visiting friends is now a serious risk, for there seems to be turkey everywhere.

Something frighteningly similar happened to myself several years ago when I arrived at a good, small hotel in Glengariff. Going to bed the first night, I jokingly said to the manageress that I would expect two grilled, freshly-caught trout for breakfast. That was exactly what I got, to the astonishment of myself and my companion. For lunch he got magnificent roast beef, but I got two more for the evening meal. Next morning – what? Two grilled trout.

We had a car and I suggested to my companion that we should take a trip to Killarney, which we did, and had lunch of lobster. Back in Glengariff again. Next morning I got my two trout. We mitched again at lunchtime. I was determined not to climb down in that hotel but a stay that had been planned for eight days was cut down to four.

Consider that king of all freshwater fish, the salmon. Last season there was a glut of salmon and the bottom fell out of the market. This had several unexpected results, one of which was a succession of rows in fish-and-chips shops. The seasoned customer, when served with his order, stared at it, stirred it and then sent for the boss.

What was this he was getting, he asked. 'My dear sir,' the boss replied proudly, 'for once in my life I'm not serving ray. That's REAL FRESH SALMON!' His market research (if we may call it that) was poor. The customer said he had ordered fish and chips, fish and chips was what he wanted, and if this happened again, he would take his custom elsewhere. And he stiffly departed, having eaten nothing.

Quite recently I read a nostalgic article about fishing on the Boyne, and how sadly it had declined since the good old days. An old document was quoted showing that in the contracts of service of the men employed on the fisheries (presumably at netting operations) they should not be expected to have salmon in the meals supplied oftener than twice a week.

It is not easy to explain why some foods – particularly

attractive, expensive, festive foods – tend to pall in this fashion with only moderate over-supply. And it is just as hard to know why the more commonplace things can be placed on the table day after day for ever and ever – bread, butter, cakes, biscuits, marmalade, potatoes, beef, lamb, rashers, eggs – without anybody making the slightest comment or objection.

What about tea, particularly in rural Ireland? The pot is *always* on the hob in some homes, and even the postman is asked in for a cup when he calls. Appetite for tea cannot apparently ever be saturated, and that applies to all ages and sexes.

There is another drink and I have seen men capable of taking plenty of it every day, every night as well, sometimes, and go to immense trouble to get it when it is not handy – or handed out: I mean whiskey. It never even occurs to them to change over to tea, though they probably know that tea can be immensely improved with a little whiskey in it.

There is quite a to-do at present about still another article that does not confer disgust with over indulgence in it. Yes, indeed. Have you got a match?

Looking back a little

This is 1964. If you doubt me, reader, take a look at the extreme top of this page. I have been looking over some old newspapers and magazines and find it hard to believe that very nearly a quarter of a century has passed since World War II was declared.

Many people reading this had not been born in 1939, and as many again had not been thought of in the sense that their parents had not yet met. It makes myself feel very oiled: very old, I mean. Those war years were an extraordinary time in Ireland and we were, of course, merely on the edge of the real thing.

We were living in a grim sort of fairyland, not really understanding the enormous issue then being decided, not realising the fabulous slaughter that was in progress at various fronts, and certainly unaware that 6 million Jews were being quietly exterminated in Germany. By 'we' I mean those of us who stayed at home: a great number of younger people departed to take a hand in the bloody game, and not all of them returned.

The homeland memory that survives is one of bleakness, uncertainty, rationing of essentials, black marketeering, the ascendency of the chancer, and the infiltration of Irish society by a great number of the young 'conchie' brigade from Britain. Only in retrospect does one realise how precarious that neutrality of ours was.

It is curious that in a situation of momentous climax for the world, it was trivialities which stand out in the mind here. Cigarettes were scarce: one had to have the leg of a tobacconist to get as many as five on demand, served loose. Simple essentials such as bread, butter, eggs, bacon and beef were rationed. Did I say bread?

This was a grey, crumbling substance apparently compounded of barnyard corn, concrete, sweepings from barbers' shops and coke. The national newspapers consisted of four pages of very condensed matter printed on grey 'paper' which had a faintly unpleasant smell.

Petrol was, of course, very strictly rationed on a coupon basis and none allowed to anybody who was not on 'essential service', which everybody tried to be. To get a gallon costing 3/6, you had first to buy a coupon costing up to 7/6 on the black market. To ask a pump attendant for a gallon without having a coupon was equivalent to asking him for a gallon of his blood.

Yet there was one class who never weakened, and that was the civil servants. It is somehow refreshing to read the reply received by a British citizen who applied to the Board of Trade for permission to have two pockets in the trousers of a suit instead of the three officially authorised, and to have the third pocket transferred to the jacket. I give the reply below, as it appeared in *The Investors' Chronicle and Market Review* under the heading 'The Blight of Bureaucracy'.

'I am to refer to your letter dated March 1 in which you make application for a licence to permit of a suit being made having more pockets than those laid down in the above-mentioned Order.

'It is noted that you do not require more than two pockets in the trousers and that you would like, instead of the third pocket, to have an extra pocket in the jacket. I am to say that the Board are not prepared to consider the giving up of one pocket in one garment sufficient reason for the granting of an extra pocket in another garment since the restrictions are imposed on the separate garment and not on the suit as a whole.

'The Board realise, however, that in certain circumstances it may be necessary to vary the restrictions and if you will state why you are unable to make use of the third pocket in the trousers (it is not necessary that this pocket should be a hip pocket, the restrictions do not in any way refer to the position of the pockets but only to the total number in each garment) thus necessitating the

221

extra jacket pocket, full consideration will be given to the issue of a licence. It would also be helpful if you would state the exact use to which the extra pockets in the jacket and waistcoat are to be put.

'With regard to your request for a small sub-division to the right-side pocket of the jacket, I am to say that this is not regarded as an extra pocket and that no licence will therefore be necessary in respect of this requirement.'

Brave words don't you think, when Britain had her BACK TO THE WALL.

Those forty days

It was very sudden but the surprise is over now – we all know that we are in the season of Lent. One of the desirable objectives which Vatican Council II studied was that of having a fixed Easter but it is a thing not yet achieved.

Two common words of which hardly anybody knows the real meaning are LENT and FASTING. Lent is a Saxon word which means just Spring, and fasting does not mean merely cutting out a meal during the day, or having much smaller meals: it means having absolutely nothing whatsoever to eat or drink.

Custom has, of course, modified the meaning of both words. It may seem disgraceful to say that Lenten fasting is not what it used to be but even middle-aged people know that such is only the truth. I remember my own grandmother taking her strong tea absolutely black and making horrible faces; and her heroism was even greater than that, for she refused to allow any sugar in it.

But such are human quirks that I personally would be horrified at the idea of tea WITH sugar in it, and I much prefer it with hardly any milk at all. Bread without butter on it was another old-time privation and as for meat, every day was a Friday. Many of those alive today and youngish will murmur, 'Ah, but the people of those times were far stronger and healthier.' Were they, though?

They certainly worked harder and what they earned for a hard week's work would hardly pass for pocket money today. Let us agree they were tougher, and had a more pronounced development in the region of the spine.

Severity

Lent itself as a fixed period of deliberate hardship was not always the settled thing we have today. In the early days of the Church the fast in preparation for Easter and some other important occasions was very short but very severe, sometimes being a total fast.

Originally the Easter fast was confined to Holy Week, and the forty-day fast (Quadragesima) was not formally laid down until the Council of Nicaea in 325 but for many centuries there was an absence of uniformity, and purely local customs of fasting, varying enormously in duration and severity, predominated throughout Christendom.

In the Middle Ages milk, eggs and meat were prohibited during Lent not only by the Church but by civil law. And diet was not the only matter on which the season of penitence turned; women wore mourning, right up to and including the court of Elizabeth I. Even in the confusion following the Reformation, observance of Lent did not wither away; the Anglican Church tried to preserve it, as did John Wesley.

It may be mentioned that fasting, as a method of self-denial, penance and purification, is by no means a Christian invention; it has been common in many cultures and religions, with great variety in the motives behind it. Fasting after a death, for instance, has been common, whether to placate the ghost of the departed or to make a sort of sacrificial occasion of the break.

Fasting has often been resorted to as an urgent form of prayer to secure something urgently needed such as a good harvest, shoals of fish, or even good weather, or – on the negative side – to avert a plague or some threatened natural disaster.

The rules of fast and abstinence, in Lent as well as out of it, could be straightforward and rigid in a primitive agricultural society. Nowadays in the complexity of modern life, where enormous numbers of people are huddled together in cities and communally employed in factories, workshops and offices, it is recognised that it is physically impossible or nearly so for the individual to order his personal affairs in matters of eating or attending religious observances on workdays.

Psychological and neurotic obstacles abound; large numbers who seek a dispensation from the fast get it, and we cannot guess how many grant a dispensation to themselves; it is usually enough that a person who has a wakeful conscience does not ignore it but devises exercises in self-denial which may in fact be much more onerous than those prescribed.

And here we are back, I am afraid, to smoking. Long before the lung cancer scare was heard of, it was quite usual for tens of thousands of heavy smokers to cut out cigarettes completely during Lent – and without reading books on how to do it, consulting psychoanalysts or taking pills guaranteed to make cigarettes taste poisonous.

And there are plenty of them still with us and they still cannot explain why they joyfully light up again on Easter Saturday, even though they have completely broken the habit.

Perhaps somebody should compile a complete new form of abstinence, or several from which to choose. Suppose you determined during Lent never to look at a newspaper or listen to a radio news bulletin? to say not one word more than is necessary?

To wash the dishes after every meal in your own house (if you happen to be a husband)? To pick on something you loathe – e.g., factory-made raspberry jam – and have it at every meal? Read half a novel by Dickens every day? As often as possible sit through films you know you've seen before?

I am afraid original people trying out such systems would be disseminating Lent – making others as well as themselves suffer, ending up perhaps by causing a breach of the peace.

O'Casey ploughs again

There is something vaguely comic about the re-appearance of *The Plough and the Stars* on the stage of the Abbey Theatre, advertised by the management as being 'by special permission' of Sean O'Casey.

When the theatre refused a new play of his, *The Bishop's Bonfire,* over six years ago, reportedly because it was anti-clerical, the playwright got into a huff or a tantrum or a pet, and excommunicated the theatre with truly ecclesiastical solemnity.

O'Casey likes to consider himself as an equal of Bernard Shaw but in a like situation Shaw would hardly have taken himself so seriously; very likely he would have contented himself with sending off a scurrilous postcard. It seems that O'Casey has now relented as a result of the Abbey Company being invited to play in London in connexion with the quartercentenary of the birth of Shakespeare.

The attitude of many people, Dubliners included, to the Abbey Theatre has changed a lot in recent years. Most of the great players of the past are dead or departed, and new plays of real stature are apparently not forthcoming. Moreover, there has been a policy of gaelicisation which many feel is out of tune with the theatre's origin.

When a play in Irish is on, the programme refers to the stalls as 'steallaí'. Probably this word has been mined out of Dinneen but why, I ask, don't they use the obvious word 'stol'? I might as well be talking to the wall, of course, though this phrase has always seemed pointless in view of the belief that walls have ears.

For years there has been on the programme and outside the house a phrase which annoys most people, if only for its decrepit syntax and obscurity – 'Late-comers not admitted until end of First Act.'

It has several undesirable implications: first, that every play must have not only acts but have even a first act! (Nay, a First Act.) What would, say, Rouault or some other abstract artist think of such unenterprise? Is it also suggested that every play must also have a last act?

In my youth I wrote some plays myself and competent people who read them swore that there was neither beginning nor end to them. Some of them had no characters – I did not say CHARACTER, mind – and others were without 'climaxes', 'plots' and other dreary journeyman paraphernalia, but the scripts had clearly marked pauses for applause.

The second deplorable implication of the 'late-comer' slogan is that while those who are in at the beginning will not be disturbed during the first act, they will not necessarily be undisturbed during subsequent acts. (There are bars on the present premises, remember.)

You can't barge in in the middle of the first act but you can arrive in the middle of the second or third act, start tuning the piano, decide you haven't enough light and stagger out with the thing on your back. What they really mean, you say, is 'Patrons not admitted between the acts.'

But not quite; because if that were the rule, nobody would ever get in. The . . . interval, shall we call it, before the first act could not be fairly included as 'between the acts'.

But sheer admittance to the building is not necessarily a control of disturbing the audience. After a customer has patiently endured the first half of the first act, he may decide he has had as much as he can bear, get up, disturb everybody along the row, distract the players on the stage, and stumble out. Even if he likes the play, he may be overcome by a deadly craving for a cigarette, and create a similar fuss to get out. Without leaving his seat at all, he can create havoc by falling asleep to the accompaniment of thunderous snores, or be thoroughly objectionable by arriving with, not a box of chocolates, but a bag of walnuts and proceed to crack them against each other in a mighty fist.

And, anyway, wouldn't the odd late-comer be better for everybody than several early-comers who have whooping cough?

On the whole, the Abbey should think of a more precise and literate slogan, something catchy – like this:

> The National Theatre Society
> Likes the promptness and sobriety,
> No patron will be admitted
> Unless promptly stalled (or pitted).

The real trouble is, of course, that too many of the patrons have learnt their manners from characters on the Abbey stage. I wonder has Sean O'Casy a clear conscience here? If Joxer Daly was ever in a drawing-room, he slept, cooked his dinner and drank his porter there and the house, alas, was a decayed tenement.

An oldtimer's thoughts

Most people are, like myself, fond of old books. Probably we feel that our forefathers, having arrived earlier, must have been wiser and that we miserable moderns can improve ourselves by reading what they left behind them.

I have been looking through an old book with the commonplace title of 'Information for Everybody', published in Boston, USA, in 1851. The author's name is given as Dr Chase – just this, with no Christian name and no clue as to whether he might be an ancestor of Senator Margaret Chase Smith, this year a contender for the US Presidency.

Dr Chase says that his book is Consisting of a Large Number of Medical Recipes: Also, Practical Recipes for Merchants, Grocers, Shopkeepers, Physicians, Drug-gists, Tanners, Shoemakers, Harness-Makers, Painters, Jewellers, Blacksmiths, Tinners, Gunsmiths, Farriers, Cabinet-Makers, Dyers, Barbers, &c.

That's a modern weakness – that '&c.' He shoves it in when he has absolutely failed to think of a single other word he can add to the list.

Most of his recipes are technical and boring but he invented a potion which he called 'Soot Coffee'. Hear his own words on how to make it:

Soot Coffee has cured many cases of ague after 'everything else' had failed; it is made as follows: soot scraped from a chimney (that from stove pipes does not do), 1 tablespoon steeped in water 1 pint, and settled with 1 egg beaten up in a little water, as for other coffee, with sugar and cream, 3 times daily with meals, in place of other coffee . . .

Thereafter the Doctor turns aside to castigate people, including 'Upstart Physicians' who stick up their noses at 'old grandmother prescriptions'. I agree with him there, for a lot of what nowadays is called folk medicine has a sound basis. I would gladly try this soot coffee myself if I had a chimney – or can it be that I have already had a cup of it in a certain place in Carlow at the cost of a shilling? For ague you take it with cream. Taken black, it would probably be good for nerves or a sore head, but taken any way at all it would be bound to be very good for smoky chimneys.

But Dr Chase is not just an old scientist. He has a stern moral eye, and there's many a young fellow who could take a leaf out of the Doctor's book with advantage. Here is a note he has on the drink situation, in his day very bad:

It will be seen that every quart of fruit wine not made for medicine helps to build up the cause (intemperance) which we all so much desire not to encourage. And for those who take any kind of spirit for the sake of the spirit, let me give you the following:
2. *Spiritual Facts* – That *whis-key* is the *key* by which many gain entrance into our prisons and almshouses.
3. That *brandy brands* the noses of all who cannot govern their appetites.
4. That *punch* is the cause of many unfriendly *punches.*
5. That *ale* causes many *ailings*, while *beer* brings to the *bier.*
6. That *wine* causes many to take a *winding* way home.
7. That *cham-pagne* is the source of many real *pains.*
8. That *gin-slings* have 'slewed' more than *slings* of old.

A most impressive person, the Doctor, for here are met wit, good counsel, and a lofty literary style. It is perhaps significant that the admonition numbered ONE does not appear anywhere in the text. What good thing is thereby lost it is hard to say. Probably something like '*Porter* is the man who carries the bags under your eyes.' Or better, perhaps: 'A pint of *plain* will make you very plain.' Or maybe just '*Stout* makes you very stout, no doubt.'

My own dreadful weakness is that lager makes me swagger.

Our national feast-day

Narrow green lines to guide traffic on the streets, emerald green beer in the pubs and beaming negroes wearing shamrock – that is Saint Patrick's Day for you in New York. Apart from its religious significance, the day has for long been taken very quietly indeed in Ireland.

In Dublin there is usually a considerable collision at Croke Park and, in the morning, a great procession honouring Irish manufacturers. Some of these processions in the past have been in some respects surprising and shoddy.

I have seen our national electricity undertaking publicly flexing its muscle by displaying a considerable piece of machinery (a transformer or something) on the heavy duty lorry, though surely it was made in Stuttgart? Surely a nice stretch of native bog tastefully arranged on a float would be more appropriate nowadays?

How Irish are cigarettes made in Dublin but with alien tobacco handled by foreign machines? The more one ponders this problem the more one is driven to the conclusion that there are hardly any manufactured articles in the country which are Irish from top to bottom except stout and whiskey. For that reason it was surely ironical when the first native Government evinced an unsuspected puritanical trait and ordered the complete closing of all pubs on the National Festival, giving the day the same penitential mood as Good Friday.

Drink could be had in hotels, of course, and at the famous Dublin Dog Show, but the Plain Man was denied even a pint of plain. Happily, a more enlightened view now prevails, though it happens that abstinence is still promoted by the shocking price that is now demanded for the stuff. One wonders what Saint

Patrick himself would have thought of it all.

Saint Patrick himself is an extraordinarily shadowy figure, several responsible scholars maintain that he never existed, and it is true that primitive Christianity abounds in mythical figures.

Reputedly he was born in Britain about 389, was kidnapped by marauders and brought to Ireland as a slave, escaped home and then went to France. After returning home he had a vision, went back to France to study at Auxerre and arrived in Ireland in 432. It was to commemorate that landing that we had a Eucharistic Congress here in 1932.

There is no authentic account of what Patrick did here after he arrived or whom he met, though tradition and legend are plentiful enough. But two things are reasonably certain: Christianity was in existence in Ireland before Patrick's time, and there is therefore no substance in the claim that it was he who first brought the new message here; secondly, Pope Celestine had already sent Palladius, who had laboured in Britain to stamp out the Pelagian heresy, to Ireland to do the same thing.

The only surviving document definitely ascribed to Patrick is the Confession, which appears in the Book of Armagh, said to date from about 800; it gives a general account of his career but is couched in Latin that is crude at best, and sometimes downright bad.

There are, of course, other and far later accounts of Patrick's life but it is hard to understand the absence of reliable contemporary information, having regard to how minutely we know the people of a far earlier day – the Apostles, for example, or all the kings and prophets of the Old Testament.

Most people would be appalled by the theory that Saint Patrick never existed and that he is simply a pious myth, as was shown a few years ago and acknowledged by the Holy See in the case of Saint Philomena. But there is an even worse possibility. A learned historian and philologist named Professor D.A. Binchy has been maintaining for many years, both in writing and lecture hall, that in fact there were TWO Saint Patricks!

This is hardly the place to set forth his arguments and the sources on which he relies but it can be said that his theory has never been refuted. However unlikely, it is possible that another *savant* may yet come along and establish that there were three of them.

However tenuous the proof, most people – but particularly the Americans – will be glad to settle for one Saint Patrick and beg leave to inquire no further. Imagine . . . just imagine . . . where we would be if we were to have two Saint Patrick Days every year.

The Irishman would then cut a queer figure in the world: people would stare at him as if he had two heads!

'Buy home products'

Well, we've had another St Patrick's Day, with all attendant shamrockry, champagne and shenanigans. The Saint has been once again toasted all over the world, and for at least a week in Ireland the motto has been BUY IRISH (but with no sly reference to whiskey hidden in the phrase). How real and how true is all this? Do we mean it? Do others mean it? Or is the cult of Saint Patrick an internationally-accepted sham, like Santa Claus?

At the outset, I honestly say I don't know. But I have genuine cause for wonder.

Last week I went into a tavern on purpose to have a snack. I won't say where, but it was not in Carlow town. It was a pleasant enough house. I sat at the fire and ordered bread and butter, some sardines and a bottle of ale. The bottle of ale was British, because the native article stocked was not in condition. The butter, rather like cheese, was Danish. The sardines came from Norway. The coal in the fire was American. The knife was made in Sheffield, and I assume the bread was made from imported grain. And do we manufacture salt here? I don't think so.

You might imagine that we could go no further than that? Wrong!

I stood up and turned my chair upside down. (I thought standing up was a desirable preliminary.) *Hurrah!* There was an inscription on the underside of the seat in the bold characters of the old tongue, namely, '*Déanta sa Phólain*'.

The phrase means 'Made in Poland'.

Taking a sad farewell, I was nearly run over by an American car burning Iranian petrol.

Who made the paper, the ink, the machinery that enables you to read this? But perhaps I am asking too

234

many questions this week.

But talking of pubs, I think we are inclined to take too much for granted. A public house looks simple but isn't. I have been looking through a publication issued by Messrs Guinness entitled *Handbook for Customers* and I find there is nothing simple or obvious about the bottle of stout or its management. The tapping of a cask (the *Handbook* carelessly calls this thing indiscriminately Cash and cask) is a difficult and esoteric process. To begin with you have to put the cask 'lying on a stillion, bung up'. There is later the question of the Keystone Plug, which must receive 'one hard blow'. Later comes along a 'Starter', possibly with a pistol in his hand. The book says:

> With a starter, drive the oak shive which is in the taphole about half an inch into the cask. (If any difficulty is found in doing this, not more than a quarter of an inch of the shive may be removed by a chisel before using the Starter.)

Do you know what is meant by venting a cask? The instructions are a bit obscure, but venting is a process definitely carried out by licensed vintners.

Before bottling its contents a cask must be rolled to 'rouse' the beer. Also, 'strict cleanliness is necessary to good bottling' – I would prefer 'for' instead of 'to' there, nor do I know the distinction between cleanliness and strict cleanliness. Yet perhaps there is a distinction. If one publican gives a hot bath to his cellar-rats once a week while another does it every day, I suppose their standards cannot be identical. The *Handbook* is unbending on one particular. 'Cullet and rubbish must be removed,' it says, with severity in its steely prose. What on earth is this Cullet? Could it be the name of some nasty old man? I have looked up the telephone book and find there is not a single Cullet in the country to ring up in search of information.

There is a whole section devoted in the *Handbook* to Crown Corks. Guinness is a London company, but they go a bit far, I feel, with this hint that they get their corks from Buckingham Palace.

A last thought; nearly a year must roll by before we have another St Patrick's Day. Can we stand the strain of waiting?

What's our address?

I am sure the reader has noticed the slow but inexorable change by common usage of the name of this unkingly territory from Eire to Republic of Ireland. I am not very clear why the handier Irish Republic is so studiously avoided but it is clear that 'Eire' is pretty universally disliked.

I heard through my grapevine that there was a devil of a row between a Government department and the designers of the Irish stand at the New York World Fair about what the country's name was; only after a bitter battle did the designers succeed in establishing the fact that where we live is IRELAND.

The Eire label is set forth in the Constitution. Is it the best name? I doubt it, mind you. We had others in the old days, of course, when the old crowd were around. Banba, for instance, now hyphenated Ban-ba in honour of their Excellencies, the Censorship Board.

Then we had Scotia. This title has been lifted by British Railways for one of their mailboats, so we can hardly use it again. In any case there is now a Nova Scotia and, if anything, we would have to be Antica Scotia. (Not, hasty reader, Antiqua; for that word refers to time, the other to space. Antica Scotia means the foremost Scotia.)

Another name we had was Fodhla, which sounds like a baby food. I'm no longer interested in baby foods though I'm told that some people named Power do very well out of them. 'Hibernia' is notable only for the fact that the well-known quotation means that the visiting team became more wintry than the Irish themselves, not more Irish.

'Saorstát Éireann' was still another pseudonym adopted by this most honourable Irish nation. 'Saor', of course, means 'mason' and I have always held that the

SE title attributed undue influence to the Masons in our national affairs. The only other title that occurs to me at the moment is the one used among ourselves, in privacy of family or public house circle: I mean 'this b—country'.

What about rethinking the thing, and having the name properly changed? It would mean a referendum, of course, but unless we have more frequent appeals to the people, I fear the traditional science of personation will be a thing of the past, like 'patterns', homespuns, rinnkeh faudas, potheen and efficient public transport.

'Eire' is over-full of vowels (75 per cent in fact) which means that the word is open to crazy mispronunciations on the part of foreigners. Could we not call this country . . . Cork? (Go on, laugh. What is wrong with my suggestion, anyway?)

Cork is a simple word that is known the world over for cuteness, alcoholism and literary posturing. The crowd down there have got a bad name for the whole lot of us and I hold that our national ignominy should be geographically located and acknowledged. A town such as Cork, which holds that the rest of Ireland is provincial, deserves to be freed from a name that means 'swamp' – if only to utilise, for national purposes, the paranoia, the secret studying, the shrewd marriage, the innumerable small forethoughts that have made our higher executive officers the finest in the world.

Call the country Cork and the other place Eire. Think of the distinction for your children unborn – they will be Corkmen one and all! And therefore they will write 'novels'! Even we who are now alive could become naturalised Corkmen!

I had a vision, or nightmare, the other night. Dreamt I went up to the Patents Office in Dublin Castle to try to patent being Irish. I had drawn up a very detailed specification. You see, I want this unique affectation protected by world right. I am afraid of my life that other people will find out that being Irish pays and start invading our monopoly.

I am not sure that certain sections of the population in America have not already infringed our immemorial rights in this regard. I did not get very far with the stupid officials I saw.

They held that copyright did not subsist in being Irish and more or less suggested that it was open to any man to be Irish if he chose, and to behave in an Irish way. I pointed to the Cork colony, who were regarded by the rest of Ireland merely as Corkmen. No use.

The officials made the dastardly suggestion that even Corkmen could be regarded as Irishmen . . . of a kind. It was only on my way out that I realised the reason for this extraordinary attitude. Funny how the Coal Quay breaks out through the whitest official shirt.

Marching schoolboys

As I write, we have the ironic spectacle of young fellows on the march in Dublin demanding the safeguarding of schoolboys' rights and their ancient entitlement to undergo examinations. Perhaps by the time this is printed somebody will have climbed down. But perhaps what one might call the pathology of literacy and literature is worth looking at.

What prompts a sane inoffensive man to write? Assuming that to 'write' is mechanically to multiply communication (though that is sometimes a strong assumption), what vast yeasty eructation of egotism drives a man to address simultaneously a mass of people he has never met, people who may resent being pestered with his 'thoughts'? They don't have to read what he writes, you say? But they do. That is, indeed, the more vicious neurosis that calls for inquiry. The blind urge to read, the craving for print – that is an infirmity so deeply seated in the mind today as to be almost ineradicable. People blame compulsory education and Lord Northcliffe. The writer can be systematically discouraged, his 'work' can be derided and, if all else fails, in a military society the creative intellectuals can be liquidated. But what can you do with the passive print addict? Very little.

Average Day

Consider the average day of the average man who is averagedly educated. The moment he opens his eyes he reads that extremely distasteful and tragic story that is to be found morning after morning on the face of his watch. Late again. He is barely downstairs when he has thrown open (with what is surely the pathetic abandon of a person who knows he is lost) that white tablet of lies, his newspaper. He assimilates his literary narcotic in silence, giving only 5 per cent of his attention to the business of eating. His wife has ruined her sight from trying for years to read the same paper upside-down from the other side of the table, and he must therefore leave it behind him when he rushes out to his work. Our subject is nervous on his way, his movements are undecided; he is temporarily parted from his drug. Notice how advertisements he has been looking at for twenty years are frenziedly scrutinised, the books and papers of neighbours on the bus carefully scanned, even the bus ticket meticulously perused. Clocks are read and resented.

At last the office is reached. Hurrah! Thousands of documents – books, papers, letters, calendars, memos, diaries, threats to sue, bailiffs' writs! Writing, type-script, PRINT! Heaven at last – an orgy of myopic indulgence! Consider the countless millions who sit in offices all day throughout the world endlessly writing to each other, endlessly reading each other's writings! Ink-wells falling and falling in level as words are extracted from them by the hundred thousand! Tape-machines, dictaphones, typewriters and printing presses wearing out their metal hearts to feed this monstrous lust for unspoken words!

And now consider that rare and delightful soul (admittedly he lives mostly in the Balkans) – the illiterate. Think of his quiet personal world, so untroubled by catastrophes, threats of war, cures for heart disease, the fact that it is high water at Galway at 2.47 p.m., or even the death at an advanced age of a distinguished prelate who had reflected the light of heaven on his flock for 53 years. Recall the paragraph of a brother-scribe of mine who saw a poor countryman 'reading' the morning paper upside-down and remark-ing that there was another big one sunk as he gazed at the picture of an inverted liner. Think of the illiterate's acute observation of the real world as distinct from the pale, print-interpreted thing that means life for most of us.

If you know such a person, leave him to his happiness. Do not pity him or patronise him, for he is suffering from nothing more terrible than innocence. Of all the things you read yourself, you know the great majority are unpleasant, sad or worrying. And if you can read, reflect that your accomplishment is irreversible. You cannot discard it as you would an old jacket that is a bit tattered and no longer fits properly. Those marching schoolboys will have many a chance later on to reflect soundly on those exams that they once got so excited about. ABC is the beginning of pain and boredom.

Some are 'out of line'

I am sure many people were amused at the suggestion made in the Dáil last week by Mr 'Pa' O'Donnell (FG) that a book on etiquette should be compiled for use in our schools and for circulation to adults through the libraries.

It would be troublesome and tedious to decide which one of all the legislative assemblies in the world merits a gold-plated cup for being in its proceedings the most unmannerly, scurrilous and reeking with insults and contumely but it is a sure thing that Dáil Éireann would be very high up on the list.

I speak as one who had to frequent Leinster House for many years, and my memories are grim. Language apart, it is a fundamental of politeness in a man joining a company or exhibiting himself in public that he should be presentable in his person and recently washed.

It is only their familiarity with them on the part of the ushers and Guards that prevents the arrest of many shabby, unshaven, often tieless characters who may be seen in the corridors and bar, and even occasionally getting up to speak in the chamber.

But as usual I can come to the rescue. I have a book called *Etiquette for Men* by G.R.M. Devereux and published in the last century. Today I will give readers some of the pithy maxims at the end of the book; some of them may seem a wee bit dated but no true *Nationalist* reader can fail to benefit.

Don't wear a low hat or a straw with a frock, or tail coat.

Don't clean or pare your nails anywhere but in your own room.

Don't caress your moustache incessantly, however

243

delicate or robust its growth; nothing is more annoying or unpleasant to those who have to witness it, or makes the owner of the appendage look more silly.

Don't take down a whole glass of wine at one gulp.

Don't mash your food all up together on your plate.

Don't turn your meat over continually on your plate, as though examining it. Avoid all appearance of wrestling with your food.

Don't produce your own cigar or cigarettes at a dinner party, and smoke them in preference to those of your host.

Don't make noises with your mouth when eating or drinking.

Don't keep your mouth open while eating or listening or at any time.

Don't refrain from offering your seat for fear of your offer being accepted.

Don't use a toothpick in public; it is a disgusting habit.

Don't break your bread and drop pieces in the soup.

Don't turn an egg out into a glass or cup to eat it; an egg should be eaten with the utmost daintiness.

Don't say 'good-afternoon' or 'good day' when taking leave of your host, a friend, or anyone who is your equal. 'Good-bye' is the correct term.

Don't turn your trousers up at the bottom, unless there is real mud about.

Don't stir the fire with your foot, or put coal on with your fingers.

I am leaving two of the most striking admonitions to the end, but meantime, dear reader, have you noticed anything peculiar about the foregoing prohibitions? They have one quality, explicit in some and implicit in them all. Look over them again, if you like.

Got it? *They are addressed exclusively to men!* I suppose it would be risky to assume that all ladies were so well brought up in those days that they were in no need of advice. Victoria, if I am correctly informed, was a very grumpy old lady, and indeed she used to sit, very brazenly, outside Leinster House. But here are the last two massive don'ts:

Don't speak of an umbrella as an umber-ella, nor of a brougham as a broo-ham; never sound the H.

Don't sound the L in golf; speak of it as goff, not gauff.

You could set the last one to music, recording it in tonic soffa!

Ah, barefoot days!

It is not because my hands are full but this week I would like to talk, if I may, about my feet. I am wondering if what I have to say will awake an echo in some reader's mind?

When the world was trying to recover from the Great War I was a young fellow in Dublin, a bold strap of a chisler, on the brink of being sent to school, and I would say that my people – what I wouldn't have dared to have said then – were lower middle class. That connotes, of course, ultra respectability, carefulness amounting to perhaps contempt for the real poor. Yes, a lot of us were like that!

Such families were subject to all kinds of fads. Many fathers believed that sugar, for instance, was very bad for a growing youngster; he was not allowed to have it at any meal, and would get a hiding if caught eating sweets. Other fathers thought that tea was poison for a youngster and totally prohibited it. Butter, white baker's bread, pork, ice cream, chocolate and goodness knows what other everyday item was also on some-body's forbidden list. It all looks very silly now in retrospect, particularly when the tiny citizens feel deprived without a supply of purple hearts or marijuana cigarettes.

But I remember one fad that simultaneously struck my own parents as well as those of practically all my hoity-toity companions. And I hesitate to call this a 'fad' because, to this day, I believe the idea was very sound, and is still very sound. Perhaps the thing started innocently and quietly enough in a newspaper article but I know it spread through our people like wildfire. The theory was that boots or shoes (and shoes were a rarity in those days) should never be worn by young growing children because they distorted and deformed the little feet then in process of being shaped, and could leave a youngster permanently gammy footed for life.

So we were all ordered to go about barefoot, like dogs or cats or the birds of the air. At this remove it may sound barbarous, particularly in the case of youngsters whose neatness in dress was a matter of family pride. But I do remember that after the first few days we thought nothing of it and even the grown-ups in the street soon stopped taking notice of respectable barefoot boys, there were so many of us.

Without attempting a pun I may say that Mother Nature took this sort of thing in her stride. After quite a short time something approximating to a natural sole, thick and nerveless, began forming on the nether surface of the feet, and soon the roughest or sharpest ground did not cause the slightest pain or inconvenience; even an odd bit of broken glass could be negotiated without injury. In fact we got TOUGH.

I can't remember now, alas, when the pressure of convention forced me to resume wearing boots, or how footwear can be justified at all in view of how happily and healthily one can carry on without it. I suppose somebody will mutter something about fashion. If you look at a pair of boots or shoes coldly in the face, you will find they are awkward, cheap-looking and vulgar – certainly far from elegant. More than likely you will find they are dirty, neglected, unshined for days, possibly broken and leaking. No matter how smart and new your suit is, your whole appearance is utterly betrayed by a bad pair of shoes. And as I have said above, they are utterly unnecessary.

Some unthinking people may be horrified at the idea of adults going about their everyday business in bare feet, but that is merely the force of irrational convention, possibly allied to the secret knowledge that a lot of poor feet are not much to look at with their bunions, corns, twisted toes and broken nails. All that sort of wreckage comes from wearing shoes, for it is more than likely that the shoe that fits properly has not yet been made. Many of the fleetest runners who have run away with world records have done so in their bare feet, and all swimmers have found that it is better to leave their shoes on the shore.

Next time you have a chance, have a good look at the bare foot of a healthy, young, well-developed man: you will see that it is a thing of beauty, style, complexity and elegance, a tool of movement and power, something certainly not to be hidden away in shame. For if the human feet are ugly and shameful, why are we not also self-conscious about our hands, and blush to think of holding it out naked, to be grasped possibly by a total stranger? Our faces, too – is there not something to be said for carefully hiding some of them, as some eastern women do under their system of purdah?

It is too much to hope, I suppose, for the liberation of human feet and the passage of a statute declaring the wearing of footwear illegal. But it would be a great day for Ireland, and maybe an example to the world, if such a measure were passed by Dáil Éireann, with every man-jack of a TD sitting there with his bare spawgs outstretched, for all to see and admire.

The butt of my gut

All readers of this newspaper (well, some of them) will be delighted to see me back here and at action stations, a bigger divil than I was before.

The cause of my absence was illness, which befell me through no fault of my own.

A person who insists on telling you at great length and with enormity of repetition all about his operation is regarded the world over as a bore, but I insist on doing that because, one, my account may be of great value and warning to the reader and, two, I had TWO operations.

Grapes and Paperbacks

Think what that means. It means two sessions of pre-operative scrutiny, two trips to the table, two prolonged sessions of convalescence punctuated with presents of unripe grapes, detestable marzipan sweets, cigarettes (for me, a non-smoker!), tattered paperback books I had already read – these were all unwelcome presents from friends – plus, for 12 hours a day, the roars from two radios in my small ward, each going full blast on different stations.

I don't suppose I need add anything about being pulled out of my drugged sleep at 6 in the morning and being invited by the sweet nurse to try and wash in a basin of tepid water.

I don't think Purgatory could be worse than a term in certain hospitals, though wild horses would not drag from me the name of this particular hospital nor the names of the distinguished doctors and surgeons. But I may say it did not happen in the Counties Carlow, Kildare, Laois or Wicklow, where the people seem to be very self-conscious about hospitals.

How It Began

For some weeks I hadn't been feeling too well in myself and one night got a frightful pain in the pit of my stomach, a bit to the right-hand side. I called in the nearest local doctor, and after humming and hawing, taking my temperature and tapping me here and there, he said I was a very bad case of appendicitis, and would have to go to hospital immediately and have the appendix out.

Well, what could I say or do? Nothing but comply.

In I went and, after a day or so, the job was done. There was hardly any pain until I found myself back in bed again and woefully awake. Pain is hardly the word for that feeling in my side, and it was just awful when I happened to cough or sneeze.

The other pain (I mean the two-radio one) was almost unendurable. But in the evening time they gave me the needle – morphine, I suppose.

A Naggin

I was there 'recovering' for over a week, but, in truth, I was fading away. As the days passed I was being given more and more build-up food but continuing to look more and more like a scarecrow. Moreover, I would get terrible pains after a meal. A friend smuggled in a naggin of whiskey, but this was the price of me, for I nearly passed out.

Eventually, against the doctor's advice, I decided to get up and crawl home. If I was going to die, surely home was the proper place for that?

Last Throw

Eventually friends advised me to see a specialist, a practitioner so-called because he specialises in high fees. This man examined me and sent me into another hospital to be X-rayed. He told me afterwards that the lower part of my main gut was in a terrible state because 'some ass had cut out a perfectly healthy appendix.' Well, what could be done, I asked. He walked up and down beside the bed, pondering this.

'You see,' he said at last, 'you should have that appendix.

'Grafting on an appendix is almost unknown as a feat of surgery. It is almost certain that your body would reject somebody else's appendix. Still, if somebody very like you turned up genuinely requiring to have his appendix removed, we might risk the transplant.'

'Somebody very like me?' I queried. 'Well, I am youngish, dark, with lovely wavy hair, clean-cut features, strong, athletic figure, perfect teeth.'

Butt of My Gut

He went away at this, frowning a bit, but rushed in two days later saying that the very man had arrived, and that the operation – or rather the two operations – would be performed that evening. And so it was done. The newly severed appendix of my unknown benefactor was sewn on to the butt of my gut . . . and the transplant worked! I began to eat every bit of food I got as well as apples, plums, sticks of raw rhubarb, chickory and celery I sent out for, and was never with less than half a dozen bottles of stout under the bed. I told the two radio maniacs that if they did not close down their stations for 7 hours a day, I would get up and thrash the life out of them.

So there you are – I'm all right again. It's easy to sleep, Ernie O'Malley used to say, on another man's wound. It's even easier on another man's appendix.

Our own troubles

Well, well, well – things get tougher. Here we are in the second half of March, most of us perished with the cold or soaked to the skin (or both, maybe) and we already have the privilege of finding ourselves in Summer Time. But can we ignore watches, newspapers, schedules of TV shows and go quietly into hibernation? No, indeed! We also have a General Election on our hands. In a way, that laborious procedure could be regarded as one for the election of a General. But if now-unarmed political Generals are nowadays not so numerous as they used to be, here is a question: apart from outgoing deputies who have, or think they have, cast-iron safe seats, is there any large body of citizens in the country who actually welcome and enjoy a General Election? (I know that the question sounds like asking anybody in the hall at the large overflow meeting who is fond of whiskey, purple hearts or goof balls to raise one hand . . . but the question is serious. And the answer is YES.) Those citizens are schoolchildren of both sexes, mostly those attending national schools. It may be very cynical but on the appointed day those lyceums of lower learning are turned into polling stations; the homes of innocence temporarily become part of the grim apparatus of politics and the scheming of sundry chancers.

Open Secrets

One could write a lot about the oddities and anomalies of the Irish election. Bribery is illegal, for instance – but only in the sense of giving a voter money or an expensive 'present'. But if a candidate swears that, if elected, he will get a job with the civil service or the local authority for the voter's son, that is just harmless electioneering blather and not seriously regarded by the law. The voter's choice on the ballot paper is strictly secret, with a special little caboose within which to mark the paper, but voters are whisked to the polling station free in cars plastered with party banners. True, such voters could cheat in the sense of voting for the other party, but in fact how many do . . . and how many feel conscience-bound to repay the transportation kindness with a vote? Nobody knows the answer to that. And if the ballot is secret by law, why do so many people afflict and bore all others around them saying and emphasising for whom they are going to vote, a procedure which in some situations could lead to blows?

Consider this other thing known as canvassing. A total stranger knocks at your door and straightway begins to explain to you the nature of your public duty, and for whom you must vote. The implication is that you are a feeble-minded, pitiable person, and that you know nothing of politics. I confess that this has never happened to myself but maybe the possibility of it is one of the reasons why I keep a good dog. Election literature, as it is called, is no problem. Put it aside to help light the fire.

Does standing strong liquor to strangers in a pub constitute bribery? I can't say, but the practice is quite common with candidates, their agents, relations and chief supporters.

Would It Help?

In some ballot arrangements (e.g. the universities and professional bodies) there is postal voting. Every person on the register receives by post a ballot paper, brief memo of instruction and a reply-paid envelope for the return of the paper, duly marked. Could a General Election be managed this way? It is very doubtful, I'm afraid. In a multi-vote household, old or blank-minded persons could be intimidated, or one rogue in the family could secretly snaffle all the papers and mark them to his own way of thinking. And even to this day there must be some illiterate voters.

I have not personally taken kindly to television but heretofore decent citizens who have forked out the £5 licence fee have had to endure the interruption of programmes by silly, shoddy advertising matter. For several coming weeks they will also have to face shabby all-too-familiar politicians letting out of them spiels about agriculture, tourism, the cost of living, the warble-fly menace, the Irish language, the Border, Ireland's destiny as a world force, the right price for malting barley, the suffering poor – stuff that everybody has heard and read hundreds of times before.

I suggest that the main parties should be classified as illegal organisations.

My own policy

The reader must try to be forbearing and tolerant if I am seen to move with the times, and present this week a deluge of electioneering. True I am not standing (as the commercial traveller said during a fleeting visit to a pub in Tullow) but is that any reason why I should not give out a lot of nonsense at the top of my voice? Have I not got the same constitutional right to talk rubbish publicly as (say) MacEntee? The fact is that anybody can play at this game, and indeed the game might be improved if everybody did.

Extravagance then might be kept within reasonable limits, and wild talk might perhaps be a little bit less wild. If a candidate swears that on election he will offer me £1,500 per acre for my 25 acre farm (– I haven't got any farm) I can't see why I must not myself offer everybody £3,000 an acre, even without being a candidate at all.

At times like this a few of us take a side-long, suspicious look at this thing we call democracy. Is it all a farce, a parlour game played for the benefit of those on the make? How many affirmations of eternal service, loyalty, sleepless days and nights of cruel work, would be forthcoming if a seat in the Dáil did not carry with it a fat salary? I believe that the POSITIONS VACANT column in newspapers would have to be used to fill any position in parliament, and that the utmost inducement a candidate would offer the elector would be a promise to do his best to keep the sheriff off for 14 days. The truth is that life overtakes people – even political people. In the bar in Leinster House it is possible to order a drink *and pay for it yourself*! (Honest! I've tried it.)

My Promises

Let us assume then, that I am not going up and that you are not going up but that we insist on exercising the Walter Mitty in us all to make silly promises to which nobody can hold us. What sort of a gaudy future would you paint? How glorious would the Ireland of tomorrow be? What costly baubles would you offer the lady next door? I am not sure that I would trust you, even in the matter of meaningless boasts. Probably you would undertake to have delivered to her a set of pots and pans made of solid gold, without stopping to consider that gold has a low melting point and would be useless for cooking a breakfast with.

Why not be BIG and offer a dwelling house made entirely of 18-carat gold (which contains a fair amount of strengthening copper), a stratoflight between Shannon and New York for two years non-stop, a knockdown to Danny Kaye and a ticket for two to the races at Leopardstown on New Year's Day, 1986? Now *that* basketful should pull in a few votes, for there is nothing illegal about daydreaming.

Yet somehow I feel that human cravings have little to do with gold, parades of opulence or fairy godmothers. The things that people REALLY want vary from day to day. Yesterday I asked a friend (while I had this article in mind) what above all else he would like at that moment, both of us being seated in a bus.

'Listen,' he said. 'If you have a magic wand, prepare to wave it now. The shoe on my right foot has been cutting the life out of me since I left home this morning. I sent it to be repaired and this is what I've got. I'm sure my sock is full of blood. I'm in a desperate condition. Have you any whiskey in your pocket?'

You see? Gold was far from his mind. He wanted (foolishly) to get away from pain. That seems to show that the aspirations of humanity are modest and that they have little use for the sun, moon and stars. To reduce humanity's yearnings to an ultimate low, I think it is adequate to say that humanity wants to be left alone, particularly by politicians. Since nobody takes their vapouring seriously, why have them?

All the Same

What I have written has been at the dictate of plain reason. But since when did plain reason get anybody elected to a job with a salary? If and when I run for office, I promise every elector who votes for me

a farm of not less that 500 acres, equally suited for tillage or pasture;

a sum of £25 a week for life, without deduction of income tax;

a Rolls-Royce car, and a Mini for the missus;

malt and fags ad lib;

top jobs in the civil service for all the children;

directorship of the Bank of Ireland;

no more wet, dirty, weather;

free copies of all banned books.

That should bring the votes in all right. But – heavens! – I nearly forgot something. I also offer the elector the editorial chair of this newspaper.

How do you rate?

A Minister of State made a pronouncement on this subject after a public dinner recently. ('After a public dinner' is good, for he took good care to have the dinner before he squawked.) He said: 'This business of rates is under consideration by the Government. I don't know what to make of it.'

Those who have any dealings with public departments will know what is meant by the phrase 'under consideration'. It means that absolutely nothing whatsoever is being done about something that is acerbating the public temper to the point of open revolt. The hidden, petted, shrouded Minister does not have to worry. He pays no income tax on his salary as a TD. He knows nothing of petrol tax, for he is whisked from here to there in a Mercedes car owned by the State at absolutely no charge. Now and again in public address he lectures the citizen on the necessity for being austere, girding his loins, the necessity for stopping smoking (where an enormous chunk of State revenue resides) and what Patrick Pearse died for. The admonitions one gets from this class of politician-on-the-make make one sick. Therefore why not get sick? Me – I just don't know how to do it on the printed page!

Back to Rates

Probably no reader of these notes is immune from the horrifying demand that arrives on the doorstep twice a year. PAY UP – Or Else. It has no relation to your income, your birth or origin, your commercial worth, the colour of your face . . . nothing. Pay up to the County Council, or the Urban Council, or you'll be sold up. Your bed will be put to auction. The chair in which you sit to read this will go to the highest bidder. How do you like that for Freedom? Is this what Pearse & Co. had in 1916 and Michael Collins later?

For this philosophy of taxation it is necessary to go back to imperial Rome. There tax was imposed on the defenceless, the inert, the supine – without any regard to their capacity to pay. The rate-collector at your door does not ask whether in fact you can pay, what your income is. He wants the dough, and reminds you that the sheriff will be along if he doesn't get it.

But is there a distinction between the demand made on you be the Tax Collector and the Rate Collector? Yes, there is. It is really a different method of tickling you until you go down the Swanee, anyway.

Are you Schedule A?

The main difference between central and local taxation (i.e rates and income tax) is that the rate collector assumes you live on air. He goes further and assumes that you exist for the purpose of getting revenue for him. The income tax merchant is slightly broader in mind and allows you a 'personal allowance' and a 'married allowance' and all sorts of other comic Treasury trash. The income tax inspector at least concedes that you are alive, that you might spend money to remain alive – heavens, that you might marry! But not the rate collector. This character, a victim of wall-eye, chronic obtuseness and in the country an almost lethal round of councillors' house to get the job.

On this whole subject I suppose the exercise of reason is futile. We may tell ourselves (or each other) that we are here for the pursuit of happiness or the fulfilment of a plan entrusted to us by our father, or for selling that house at a profit of one thousand pounds.

How true is that, for heaven's sake?

Not true at all. We are here to be taxed.